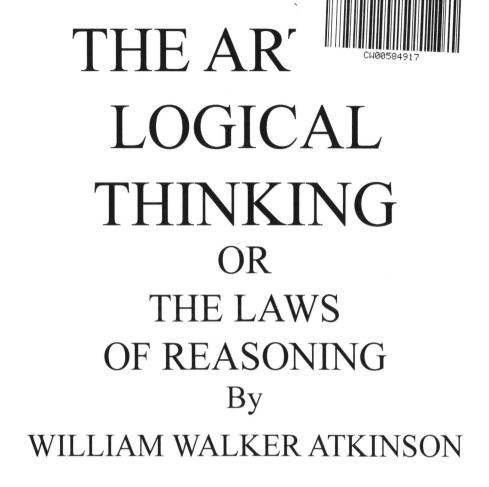

THE ART LOGICAL THINKING

OR
THE LAWS
OF REASONING

By

WILLIAM WALKER ATKINSON

Mel & Wen's
Life Transformation Publishing
Copyright © 2016

ISBN-13: 978-1530720743

ISBN-10: 1530720745

Check our website often for free ebook offers from
time to time AND we are
continually adding more titles!
240+ Book Titles & Counting!

Mel & Wen's
Life Transformation Publishing
www.lifetransformationpublishing.com
2016

Specializing in Transforming Lives!

CONTENTS

CHAPTER I.
REASONING

"Reasoning" is defined as: "The act, process or art of exercising the faculty of reason; the act or faculty of employing reason in argument; argumentation, ratiocination; reasoning power; disputation, discussion, argumentation." Stewart says: "The word reason itself is far from being precise in its meaning. In common and popular discourse it denotes that power by which we distinguish truth from falsehood, and right from wrong, and by which we are enabled to combine means for the attainment of particular ends."

By the employment of the reasoning faculties of the mind we compare objects presented to the mind as percepts or concepts, taking up the "raw materials" of thought and weaving them into more complex and elaborate mental fabrics which we call abstract and general ideas of truth. Brooks says: "It is the thinking power of the mind; the faculty which gives us what has been called thought-knowledge, in distinction from sense-knowledge. It may be regarded as the mental architect among the faculties; it transforms the material furnished by the senses ... into new products, and thus builds up the temples of science and philosophy." The last-mentioned authority adds: "Its products are twofold, ideas and thoughts. An idea is a mental product which when expressed in words does not give a proposition; a thought is a mental product which embraces the relation of two or more ideas. The ideas of the understanding are of two general classes; abstract ideas and general ideas. The thoughts are also of two general classes; those pertaining to contingent truth and those pertaining to necessary truth. In contingent truth, we have facts, or immediate judgments, and general truths including laws and causes, derived from particular facts; in necessary truth we have axioms, or self-evident truths, and the truths derived from them by reasoning, called theorems."

In inviting you to consider the processes of reasoning, we are irresistibly reminded of the old story of one of Moliere's plays in which one of the characters expresses surprise on learning that he "had been talking prose for forty years without knowing it." As Jevons says in mentioning this: "Ninety-nine people out of a hundred might be equally surprised on hearing that they had been converting propositions, syllogizing, falling into paralogisms, framing hypotheses and making classifications with genera and species. If asked whether they were logicians, they would probably answer, No! They would be partly right; for I believe that a large number even of educated persons have no clear idea of what logic is. Yet, in a certain way, every one must have been a logician since he began to speak."

So, in asking you to consider the processes of reasoning we are not assuming that you never have reasoned—on the contrary we are fully aware that you in connection with every other person, have reasoned all your mature life. That is not the question. While everyone reasons, the fact is equally true that the majority of persons reason incorrectly. Many persons reason along lines far from correct and scientific, and suffer therefor and thereby. Some writers have claimed that the majority of persons are incapable of even fairly correct reasoning, pointing to the absurd ideas entertained by the masses of people as a proof of the statement. These writers are probably a little radical in their views and statements, but one is often struck with wonder at the evidences of incapacity for interpreting facts and impressions on the part of the general public. The masses of people accept the most absurd ideas as truth, providing they are gravely asserted by some one claiming authority. The most illogical ideas are accepted without dispute or examination, providing they are stated solemnly and authoritatively. Particularly in the respective fields of religion and politics do we find this blind acceptance of illogical ideas by the multitude. Mere assertion by the leaders seems sufficient for the

5

multitude of followers to acquiesce.

In order to reason correctly it is not merely necessary to have a good intellect. An athlete may have the proper proportions, good framework, and symmetrical muscles, but he cannot expect to cope with others of his kind unless he has learned to develop those muscles and to use them to the best advantage. And, in the same way, the man who wishes to reason correctly must develop his intellectual faculties and must also learn the art of using them to the best advantage. Otherwise he will waste his mental energy and will be placed at a disadvantage when confronted with a trained logician in argument or debate. One who has witnessed a debate or argument between two men equally strong intellec-tually, one of whom is a trained logician and the other lacking this advantage, will never forget the impression produced upon him by the unequal struggle. The conflict is like that of a power-ful wrestler, untrained in the little tricks and turns of the science, in the various principles of applying force in a certain way at a certain time, at a certain place, with a trained and experienced wrestler. Or of a conflict between a muscular giant untrained in the art of boxing, when confronted with a trained and experi-enced exponent of "the manly art." The result of any such conflict is assured in advance. Therefore, everyone should refuse to rest content without a knowledge of the art of reasoning correctly, for otherwise he places himself under a heavy handicap in the race for success, and allows others, perhaps less well-equipped men-tally, to have a decided advantage over him.

Jevons says in this connection: "To be a good logician is, how-ever, far more valuable than to be a good athlete; because logic teaches us to reason well, and reasoning gives us knowledge, and knowledge, as Lord Bacon said, is power. As athletes, men can-not for a moment compare with horses or tigers or monkeys. Yet, with the power of knowledge, men tame horses and shoot tigers and despise monkeys. The weakest framework with the most logical mind will conquer in the end, because it is easy to foresee the future, to calculate the result of actions, to avoid mistakes which might be fatal, and to discover the means of doing things which seemed impossible. If such little creatures as ants had better brains than men, they would either destroy men or make them into slaves. It is true that we cannot use our eyes and ears without getting some kind of knowledge, and the brute animals can do the same. But what gives power is the deeper knowledge called Science. People may see, and hear, and feel all their lives without really learning the nature of things they see. But reason is the mind's eye, and enables us to see why things are, and when and how events may be made to happen or not to happen. The logician endeavors to learn exactly what this reason is which makes the power of men. We all, as I have said, must reason well or ill, but logic is the science of reasoning and enables us to distinguish between the good reasoning which leads to truth, and the bad reasoning which every day betrays people into error and misfortune."

In this volume we hope to be able to point out the methods and principles of correctly using the reasoning faculties of the mind, in a plain, simple manner, devoid of useless technicalities and academic discussion. We shall adhere, in the main, to the principles established by the best of the authorities of the old school of psychology, blending the same with those advanced by the best authorities of the New Psychology. No attempt to make of this book a school text-book shall be made, for our sole object and aim is to bring this important subject before the general public composed of people who have neither the time nor inclination to indulge in technical discussion nor academic hair-splitting, but who desire to understand the underlying working principles of the Laws of Reasoning.

CHAPTER II.
THE PROCESS OF REASONING

The processes of Reasoning may be said to comprise four general stages or steps, as follows:

I. Abstraction, by which is meant the process of drawing off and setting aside from an object, person or thing, a quality or attribute, and making of it a distinct object of thought. For instance, if I perceive in a lion the quality of strength, and am able to think of this quality abstractly and independently of the animal—if the term strength has an actual mental meaning to me, independent of the lion—then I have abstracted that quality; the thinking thereof is an act of abstraction; and the thought-idea itself is an abstract idea. Some writers hold that these abstract ideas are realities, and "not mere figments of fancy." As Brooks says: "The rose dies, but my idea of its color and fragrance remains." Other authorities regard Abstraction as but an act of attention concentrated upon but the particular quality to the exclusion of others, and that the abstract idea has no existence apart from the general idea of the object in which it is included. Sir William Hamilton says: "We can rivet our attention on some particular mode of a thing, as its smell, its color, its figure, its size, etc., and abstract it from the others. This may be called Modal Abstraction. The abstraction we have now been considering is performed on individual objects, and is consequently particular. There is nothing necessarily connected with generalization in abstraction; generalization is indeed dependent on abstraction, which it supposes; but abstraction does not involve generalization."

II. Generalization, by which is meant the process of forming Concepts or General Ideas. It acts in the direction of apprehending the common qualities of objects, persons and things, and combining and uniting them into a single notion or conception which will comprehend and include them all. A General Idea or Concept differs from a particular idea in that it includes within itself the qualities of the particular and other particulars, and accordingly may be applied to any one of these particulars as well as to the general class. For instance, one may have a particular idea of some particular horse, which applies only to that particular horse. He may also have a General Idea of horse, in the generic or class sense, which idea applies not only to the general class of horse but also to each and every horse which is included in that class. The expression of Generalization or Conception is called a Concept.

III. Judgment, by which is meant the process of comparing two objects, persons or things, one with another, and thus perceiving their agreement or disagreement. Thus we may compare the two concepts horse and animal, and perceiving a certain agreement between them we form the judgment that: "A horse is an animal;" or comparing horse and cow, and perceiving their disagreement, we form the judgment: "A horse is not a cow." The expression of a judgment is called a Proposition.

IV. Reasoning, by which is meant the process of comparing two objects, persons or things, through their relation to a third object, person or thing. Thus we may reason (a) that all mammals are animals; (b) that a horse is a mammal; (c) that, therefore, a horse is an animal; the result of the reasoning being the statement that: "A horse is an animal." The most fundamental principle of reasoning, therefore, consists in the comparing of two objects of thought through and by means of their relation to a third object. The natural form of expression of this process of Reasoning is called a Syllogism.

It will be seen that these four processes of reasoning necessitate the employment of the processes of Analysis and Synthesis, respectively. Analysis means a separating of an object of thought into its constituent parts, qualities or relations. Synthesis means the combining of the qualities, parts or relations of an object of thought into a composite whole. These two processes are found in all processes of Reasoning. Abstraction is principally analytic; Generalization or Conception chiefly synthetic; Judgment is either or both analytic or synthetic; Reasoning is either a synthesis of particulars in Induction, or an evolution of the particular from the general in Deduction.

There are two great classes of Reasoning; viz., (1) Inductive Reasoning, or the inference of general truths from particular truths; and (2) Deductive Reasoning, or the inference of particular truths from general truths.

Inductive Reasoning proceeds by discovering a general truth from particular truths. For instance, from the particular truths that individual men die we discover the general truth that "All men must die;" or from observing that in all observed instances ice melts at a certain temperature, we may infer that "All ice melts at a certain temperature." Inductive Reasoning proceeds from the known to the unknown. It is essentially a synthetic process. It seeks to discover general laws from particular facts.

Deductive Reasoning proceeds by discovering particular truths from general truths. Thus we reason that as all men die, John Smith, being a man, must die; or, that as all ice melts at a certain temperature, it follows that the particular piece of ice under consideration will melt at that certain temperature. Deductive Reasoning is therefore seen to be essentially an analytical process.

Mills says of Inductive Reasoning: "The inductive method of the ancients consisted in ascribing the character of general truths to all propositions which are true in all the instances of which we have knowledge. Bacon exposed the insufficiency of this method, and physical investigation has now far outgrown the Baconian conception.... Induction, then, is that operation by which we infer that what we know to be true in a particular case or cases, will be true in all cases which resemble the former in certain assignable respects. In other words, induction is the process by which we conclude that what is true of certain individuals of a class is true of the whole class, or that what is true at certain times will be true in similar circumstances at all times."

Regarding Deductive Reasoning, a writer says: "Deductive Reasoning is that process of reasoning by which we arrive at the necessary consequences, starting from admitted or established premises." Brooks says: "The general truths from which we reason to particulars are derived from several distinct sources. Some are intuitive, as the axioms of mathematics or logic. Some of them are derived from induction.... Some of them are merely hypothetical, as in the investigation of the physical sciences. Many of the hypotheses and theories of the physical sciences are used as general truth for deductive reasoning; as the theory of gravitation, the theory of light; etc. Reasoning from the theory of universal gravitation, Leverrier discovered the position of a new planet in the heavens before it had been discovered by human eyes."

Halleck points out the interdependence of Inductive and Deductive Reasoning in the following words: "Man has to find out through his own experience, or that of others, the major premises from which he argues or draws his conclusions. By induction we examine what seems to us a sufficient number of individual cases. We then conclude that the rest of these cases, which we have not examined, will obey the same general laws.... The premise, 'All cows chew the cud,' was laid down after a certain number of cows had been examined. If we were to see a cow twenty years hence, we should expect that she chewed her cud.... After

Induction has classified certain phenomena and thus given us a major premise, we proceed deductively to apply the inference to any new specimen that can be shown to belong to that class."

The several steps of Deductive Reasoning shall now be considered in turn as we proceed.

CHAPTER III.
THE CONCEPT

In considering the process of thinking, we must classify the several steps or stages of thought that we may examine each in detail for the purpose of comprehending them combined as a whole. In actual thinking these several steps or stages are not clearly separated in consciousness, so that each stands out clear and distinct from the preceding and succeeding steps or stages, but, on the contrary, they blend and shade into each other so that it is often difficult to draw a clear dividing line. The first step or stage in the process of thinking is that which is called a concept.

A concept is a mental representation of anything. Prof. Wm. James says: "The function by which we mark off, discriminate, draw a line around, and identify a numerically distinct subject of discourse is called conception." There are five stages or steps in each concept, as follows:

I. Presentation. Before a concept may be formed there must first be a presentation of the material from which the concept is to be formed. If we wish to form the concept, animal, we must first have perceived an animal, probably several kinds of animals— horses, dogs, cats, cows, pigs, lions, tigers, etc. We must also have received impressions from the sight of these animals which may be reproduced by the memory—represented to the mind. In order that we may have a full concept of animal we should have perceived every kind of animal, for otherwise there would be some elements of the full concept lacking. Accordingly it is practically impossible to have a full concept of anything. The greater the opportunities for perception the greater will be the opportunity for conception. In other books of this series we have spoken of the value and importance of the attention and of clear and full perception. Without an active employment of the attention, it is impossible to receive a clear perception of anything; and unless the perception has been clear, it is impossible for the mind to form a clear concept of the thing perceived. As Sir Wm. Hamilton has said: "An act of attention, that is an act of concentration, seems thus necessary to every exertion of consciousness, as a certain contraction of the pupil is requisite to every exertion of vision.... Attention, then, is to consciousness what the contraction of the pupil is to sight, or to the eye of the mind what the microscope or telescope is to the bodily eye.... It constitutes the half of all intellectual power." And Sir B. Brodie said: "It is attention, much more than in the abstract power of reasoning, which constitutes the vast difference which exists between minds of different individuals." And as Dr. Beattie says: "The force with which anything strikes the mind is generally in proportion to the degree of attention bestowed upon it."

II. Comparison. Following the stage of Presentation is the stage of Comparison. We separate our general concept of animal into a number of sub-concepts, or concepts of various kinds of animals. We compare the pig with the goat, the cow with the horse, in fact each animal with all other animals known to us. By this process we distinguish the points of resemblance and the points of difference. We perceive that the wolf resembles the dog to a considerable degree; that it has some points of resemblance to the fox; and a still less distinct resemblance to the bear; also that it differs materially from the horse, the cow or the elephant. We also learn that there are various kinds of wolves, all bearing a great resemblance to each other, and yet having marked points of difference. The closer we observe the various individuals among the wolves, the more points of difference do we find. The faculty of Comparison evidences itself in inductive reasoning; ability and disposition to analyze, classify, compare, etc. Fowler says that those in whom it is largely developed "Reason clearly and correctly from conclusions and scientific facts up to the laws which govern them; discern the known from the unknown; detect error by its incongruity with facts; have an excellent talent for comparing, explaining, expounding, criticising, exposing, etc." Prof. William James says: "Any personal or practical interest in the results to be obtained by distinguishing, makes one's wits amazingly sharp to detect differences. And long training and practice in distinguishing has the same effect as personal interest. Both of these agencies give to small amounts of objective difference the same effectiveness upon the mind that, under other circumstances, only large ones would make."

III. Abstraction. Following the stage of Comparison is that of Abstraction. The term "Abstraction" as used in psychology means: "The act or process of separating from the numerous qualities inherent in any object, the particular one which we wish to make the subject of observation and reflection. Or, the act of withdrawing the consciousness from a number of objects with a view to concentrate it on some particular one. The negative act of which Attention is the positive." To abstract is "to separate or set apart." In the process of Abstraction in our consideration of animals, after having recognized the various points of difference and resemblance between the various species and individuals, we proceed to consider some special quality of animals, and, in doing so, we abstract, set aside, or separate the particular quality which we wish to consider. If we wish to consider the size of animals, we abstract the quality of size from the other qualities, and consider animals with reference to size alone. Thus we consider the various degrees of size of the various animals, classifying them accordingly. In the same way we may abstract the quality of shape, color or habits, respectively, setting aside this quality for special observation and classification. If we wish to study, examine or consider certain qualities in a thing we abstract that particular quality from the other qualities of the thing; or we abstract the other qualities until nothing is left but the particular quality under consideration. In examining or considering a class or number of things, we first abstract the qualities possessed in common by the class or number of things; and also abstract or set aside the qualities not common to them.

For instance; in considering classes of animals, we abstract the combined quality of milk-giving and pouch-possessing which is possessed in common by a number of animals; then we group these several animals in a class which we name the Marsupialia, of which the opossum and kangaroo are members. In these animals the young are brought forth in an imperfect condition, undeveloped in size and condition, and are then kept in the pouch and nourished until they are able to care for themselves. Likewise, we may abstract the idea of the placenta, the appendage which connects the young unborn animal with the mother, and by means of which the fœtus is nourished. The animals distinguished by this quality are grouped together as the Placental Mammals. The Placental Mammals are divided into various groups, by an Abstraction of qualities or class resemblance or difference, as follows: The Edentata, or toothless creatures, such as the sloths, ant-eaters, armadillos, etc.; the Sirenia, so-named from their fancied resemblance to the fabled "sirens," among which class are the sea-cows, manatees, dugongs, etc.; the Cetacea, or whale family, which although fish-like in appearance, are really mammals, giving birth to living young which they nourish with breast-milk, among which are the whales, porpoises, dolphins, etc.; the Ungulata, or hoofed animals, such as the horse, the tapir, the rhinoceros, the swine, the hippopotamus, the camel, the deer, the sheep, the cow, etc.; the Hyracoidea, having teeth resembling both the hoofed animals and the gnawing animals, of which the coney or rock-rabbit is the principal example; the Proboscidea, or trunked animals, which family is represented by the various families of elephants; the Carnivora, or flesh-eaters, represented by various sub-families and species; the Rodentia, or gnawers; the

Insectivora, or insect feeders; the Cheiroptera, or finger-winged; the Lemuroidea, or lemurs, having the general appearance of the monkey, but also the long bushy tail of the fox; the Primates, including the monkeys, baboons, man-apes, gibbons, gorillas, chimpanzees, orangutans and Man.

In all of these cases you will see that each class or general family possesses a certain common quality which gives it its classification, and which quality is the subject of the Abstraction in considering the particular group of animals. Further and closer Abstraction divides these classes into sub-classes; for instance, the family or class of the Carnivora, or flesh-eaters, may be divided by further Abstraction into the classes of seals, bears, weasels, wolves, dogs, lions, tigers, leopards, etc. In this process, we must first make the more general Abstraction of the wolf and similar animals into the dog-family; and the lion, tiger and similar forms into the cat-family.

Halleck says of Abstraction: "In the process of Abstraction, we draw our attention away from a mass of confusing details, unimportant at the time, and attend only to qualities common to the class. Abstraction is little else than centering the power of attention on some qualities to the exclusion of others."

IV. Generalization. Arising from the stage of Abstraction is the stage of Generalization. Generalization is: "The act or process of generalizing or making general; bringing several objects agreeing in some point under a common or general name, head or class; an extending from particulars to generals; reducing or arranging in a genus; bringing a particular fact or series of facts into a relation with a wider circle of facts." As Bolingbroke says: "The mind, therefore, makes its utmost endeavors to generalize its ideas, beginning early with such as are most familiar and coming in time to those which are less so." Under the head of Abstraction we have seen that through Abstraction we may Generalize the various species into the various families, and thus, in turn, into the various sub-families. Following the same process we may narrow down the sub-families into species composed of various individuals; or into greater and still greater families or groups. Generalization is really the act of Classification, or forming into classes all things having certain qualities or properties in common. The corollary is that all things in a certain generalized class must possess the particular quality or property common to the class. Thus we know that all animals in the class of the Carnivora must eat flesh; and that all Mammals possess breasts from which they feed their young. As Halleck says: "We put all objects having like qualities into a certain genus, or class. When the objects are in that class, we know that certain qualities will have a general application to them all."

V. Denomination. Following closely upon the step of Generalization or Classification, is the step of Denomination. By Denomination we mean "the act of naming or designating by a name." A name is the symbol by which we think of a familiar thing without the necessity for making a distinct mental image upon each occasion of thought. Or, it may be considered as akin to a label affixed to a thing. As in the case of the algebraic symbols, a, b, c, x, and y, by the use of which we are able to make intricate calculations easily and rapidly, so may we use these word symbols much more readily than we could the lengthy descriptions or even the mental images of the thing symbolized. It is much easier for us to think "horse" than it would be to think the full definition of that animal, or to think of it by recalling a mental picture of the horse each time we wished to think of it. Or, it is much better for us to be able to glance at a label on a package or bottle than to examine the contents in detail. As Hobbes says: "A word taken at pleasure to serve for a mark, which may raise in our minds a thought like to some thought we had before, and which being pronounced to others, may be to them a sign of what thought the speaker had or had not, before in his mind." Mill says: "A name is a word (or set of words) serving the double purpose of a mark to recall to ourselves the likeness of a former thought and as a sign to make it known to others." Some philosophers regard names as symbols of our ideas of things, rather than of the things themselves; others regard them as symbols of the things themselves. It will be seen that the value of a name depends materially upon the correct meaning and understanding regarding it possessed by the person using it.

CHAPTER IV.
THE USE OF CONCEPTS

Having observed the several steps or stages of a concept, let us now consider the use and misuse of the latter. At first glance it would appear difficult to misuse a concept, but a little consideration will show that people very commonly fall into error regarding their concepts.

For instance, a child perceives a horse, a cow or a sheep and hears its elders apply the term "animal" to it. This term is perfectly correct, although symbolizing only a very general classification or generalization. But, the child knowing nothing of the more limited and detailed classification begins to generalize regarding the animal. To it, accordingly, an "animal" is identical with the dog or the cow, the sheep or the horse, as the case may be, and when the term is used the child thinks that all animals are similar to the particular animal seen. Later on, when it hears the term "animal" applied to a totally different looking creature, it thinks that a mistake has been made and a state of confusion occurs. Or, even when a term is applied within narrower limits, the same trouble occurs. The child may hear the term "dog" applied to a mastiff, and it accordingly forms a concept of dog identical with the qualities and attributes of the mastiff. Later, hearing the same term applied to a toy-terrier, it becomes indignant and cries out that the latter is no "dog" but is something entirely different. It is not until the child becomes acquainted with the fact that there are many kinds of creatures in the general category of "dog" that the latter term becomes fully understood and its appropriate concept is intelligently formed. Thus we see the importance of the step of Presentation.

In the same way the child might imagine that because some particular "man" had red hair and long whiskers, all men were red-haired and long-whiskered. Such a child would always form the concept of "man" as a creature possessed of the personal qualities just mentioned. As a writer once said, readers of current French literature might imagine that all Englishmen were short, dumpy, red-cheeked and irascible, and that all Englishwomen had great teeth and enormous feet; also that readers of English literature might imagine that all Frenchmen were like monkeys, and all Frenchwomen were sad coquettes. In the same way many American young people believe that all Englishmen say "Don't you know" and all Englishwomen constantly ejaculate: "Fancy!" Also that every Englishman wears a monocle. In the same way, the young English person, from reading the cheap novels of his own country, might well form the concept of all Americans as long-legged, chin-whiskered and big-nosed, saying "Waal, I want to know;" "I reckon;" and "Du tell;" while they tilted themselves back in a chair with their feet on the mantelpiece. The concept of a Western man, entertained by the average Eastern person who has never traveled further West than Buffalo, is equally amusing. In the same way, we have known Western people who formed a concept of Boston people as partaking of a steady and continuous diet of baked beans and studiously reading Browning and Emerson between these meals.

Halleck says: "A certain Norwegian child ten years old had the quality white firmly imbedded in his concept man. Happening one day to see a negro for the first time, the child refused to call him a man until the negro's other qualities compelled the child to revise his concept and to eliminate whiteness. If that child should ever see an Indian or a Chinaman, the concept would undergo still further revision. A girl of six, reared with an intemperate father and brothers, had the quality of drunkenness firmly fixed in her concept of man. A certain boy kept, until the age of eleven, trustworthiness in his concept of man. Another boy, until late in his teens thought that man was a creature who did wrong not from determination but from ignorance, that any man would change his course to the right path if he could but understand that he was going wrong. Happening one day to hear of a wealthy man who was neglecting to provide comforts for his aged mother in her last sickness, the boy concluded that the man did not know his mother's condition. When he informed the man, the boy was told to mind his own business. The same day he heard of some politicians who had intentionally cheated the city in letting a contract and he immediately revised his concept. It must be borne in mind that most of our concepts are subject to change during our entire life; that at first they are made only in a tentative way; that experience may show us, at any time, that they have been erroneously formed, that we have, abstracted too little or too much, made this class too wide or too narrow, or that here a quality must be added or there one taken away."

Let us now consider the mental processes involved in the formation and use of a concept. We have first, as we have seen, the presentation of the crude material from which the concept must be formed. Our attention being attracted to or directed toward an object, we notice its qualities and properties. Then we begin a process of comparison of the object perceived or of our perception of it. We compare the object with other objects or ideas in our mind, noting similarities and differences and thereby leading towards classification with similar objects and opposed dissimilar ones. The greater the range of other objects previously perceived, the greater will be the number of relations established between the new object or idea and others. As we advance in experience and knowledge, the web of related objects and ideas becomes more intricate and complex. The relations attaching to the child's concept of horse is very much simpler than the concept of the experienced adult. Then we pass on to the step of analysis, in which we separate the qualities of the object and consider them in detail. The act of abstraction is an analytical process. Then we pass on to the step of synthesis, in which we unite the materials gathered by comparison and analysis, and thus form a general idea or concept regarding the object. In this process we combine the various qualities discerned by comparison and analysis, and grouping them together as in a bundle, we tie them together with the string of synthesis and thus have a true general conception. Thus from the first general conception of horse as a simple thing, we notice first that the animal has certain qualities lacking in other things and certain others similar to other things; then we analyze the various qualities of the horse, recognized through comparison, until we have a clear and distinct idea of the various parts, qualities and properties of the horse; then we synthesize, and joining together these various conceptions of the said qualities, we at last form a clear general concept of the horse as he is, with all his qualities. Of course, if we later discover other qualities attached to the horse, we add these to our general synthesized concept—our concept of horse is enlarged.

Of course these various steps in the formation and use of a concept are not realized as distinct acts in the consciousness, for the processes are largely instinctive and subconscious, particularly in the case of the experienced individual. The subconscious, or habit mind, usually attends to these details for us, except in instances in which we deliberately apply the will to the task, as in cases of close study, in which we take the process from the region of the involuntary and place it in the voluntary category. So closely related and blended are these various steps of the process, that some authorities have disputed vigorously upon the question as to which of the two steps, comparison or analysis, precedes the other. Some have claimed that analysis must precede comparison, else how could one compare without having first analyzed the things to be compared. Others hold that comparison must precede analysis, else how could one note a quality unless he had his attention drawn to it by its resemblance to or difference from qualities in other objects. The truth seems to lie between the two ideas, for in some cases there seems to be a perception of some similarity or difference before any analysis or abstraction takes place; while in others there seems to be an analysis or abstraction before comparison is possible. In this book we have followed the arrangement favored by the latest authorities, but the question is still an open one to many minds.

As we have seen, the general concept once having been formed, the mind proceeds to classify the concept with others having general qualities in common. And, likewise, it proceeds to generalize from the classification, assuming certain qualities in certain classes. Then we proceed to make still further generalizations and classifications on an ascending and widening scale, including seeming resemblances less marked, until finally we embrace the object with other objects in as large a class as possible as well as in as close and limited a sub-class as possible. As Brooks says: "Generalization is an ascending process. The broader concept is regarded as higher than the narrower concept; a concept is considered higher than a percept; a general idea stands above a particular idea. We thus go up from particulars to generals; from percepts to concepts; from lower concepts to higher concepts. Beginning down with particular objects, we rise from them to the general idea of their class. Having formed a number of lower classes, we compare them as we did individuals and generalize them into higher classes. We perform the same process with these higher classes, and thus proceed until we are at last arrested in the highest class, Being. Having reached the pinnacle of generalization, we may descend the ladder by reversing the process through which we ascend."

From this process of generalization, or synthesis, we create from our simple concepts our general concepts. Some of the older authorities distinguished between these two classes by terming the former "conceptions," and reserving the term "concepts" for the general concepts. Brooks says of this: "The products of generalization are general ideas called concepts. We have already discussed the method of forming conceptions and now consider the nature of the concept itself.... A concept is a general idea. It is a general notion which has in it all that is common to its own class. It is a general scheme which embraces all the individuals of the class while it resembles in all respects none of its class. Thus my conception of a quadruped has in it all four-footed animals, but it does not correspond in all respects to any particular animals; my conception of a triangle embraces all triangles, but does not agree in details with any particular triangle. The general conception cannot be made to fit exactly any particular object, but it teems with many particulars. These points may be illustrated with the concepts horse, bird, color, animal, etc."

So we may begin to perceive the distinction and difference between a concept and a mental image. This distinction, and the fact that a concept cannot be imaged, is generally difficult for the beginner. It is important that one should have a clear and distinct understanding regarding this point, and so we shall consider it further in the following chapter.

CHAPTER V.
CONCEPTS AND IMAGES

As we have said, a concept cannot be imaged—cannot be used as the subject of a mental image. This statement is perplexing to the student who has been accustomed to the idea that every conception of the mind is capable of being reproduced in the form of a mental image. But the apparently paradoxical statement is seen as quite simple when a little consideration is given to it.

For instance, you have a distinct general concept of animal. You know what you mean when you say or think, animal. You recognize an animal when you see one and you understand what is meant when another uses the word in conversation. But you cannot form a mental image of the concept, animal. Why? Because any mental image you might form would be either a picture of some particular animal or else a composite of the qualities of several animals. Your concept is too broad and general to allow of a composite picture of all animals. And, in truth, your concept is not a picture of anything that actually exists in one particular, but an abstract idea embracing the qualities of all animals. It is like the algebraic x—a symbol for something that exists, but not the thing itself.

As Brooks says: "A concept cannot be represented by a concrete image. This is evident from its being general rather than particular. If its color, size or shape is fixed by an image, it is no longer general but particular." And Halleck says: "It is impossible to image anything without giving that image individual marks. The best mental images are so definite that a picture could be painted from them. A being might come under the class man and have a snub nose, blonde hair, scanty eyebrows, and no scar on his face. The presence of one of these individual peculiarities in the concept man would destroy it. If we form an image of an apple, it must be either of a yellow, red, green, or russet apple, either as large as a pippin or as small as a crab-apple. A boy was asked what he thought of when 'apple' was mentioned. He replied that he thought of 'a big, dark-red, apple with a bad spot on one side, near the top.' That boy could image distinctly, but his power of forming concepts was still in its infancy."

So we see that while a mental image must picture the particular and individual qualities, properties and appearances of some particular unit of a class, a concept can and must contain only the class qualities—that is, the qualities belonging to the entire class. The general concept is as has been said "a general idea ... a general notion which has in it all that is common to its own class." And it follows that a "general idea" of this kind cannot be pictured. A picture must be of some particular thing, while a concept is something above and higher than particular things. We may picture a man, but we cannot picture Man the concept of the race. A concept is not a reproduction of the image of a thing, but on the contrary is an idea of a class of things. We trust that the student will consider this point until he arrives at a clear understanding of the distinction, and the reason thereof.

But, while a concept is incapable of being pictured mentally as an image, it is true that some particular representative of a class may be held in the mind or imagination as an idealized object, as a general representative of the class, when we speak or think of the general term or concept, providing that its real relation to the concept is recognized. These idealized objects, however, are not concepts—they are percepts reproduced by the memory. It is important, however, to all who wish to convey their thought plainly, that they be able to convert their concepts into idealized representative objects. Otherwise, they tend to become too idealistic and abstract for common comprehension. As Halleck well says: "We should in all cases be ready to translate our concepts, when occasion requires, into the images of those individuals which the concept represents. A concept means nothing except in reference to certain individuals. Without them it could never have had existence and they are entitled to representation. A man who cannot translate his concepts into definite images of the proper objects, is fitted neither to teach, preach, nor practice any profession.... There was, not long ago, a man very fond of talking about fruit in the abstract; but he failed to recognize an individual cranberry when it was placed before him. A humorist remarked that a certain metaphysician had such a love for abstractions, and such an intense dislike for concrete things, as to refuse to eat a concrete peach when placed before him."

In the beginning many students are perplexed regarding the difference between a percept and a concept. The distinction is simple when properly considered. A percept is: "the object of an act of perception; that which is perceived." A concept is: "a mental representation." Brooks makes the following distinction: "A percept is the mental product of a real thing; a concept is a mere idea or notion of the common attributes of things. A percept represents some particular object; a concept is not particular, but general. A percept can be described by particulars; a concept can be described only by generals. The former can usually be represented by an image, the latter cannot be imagined, it can only be thought." Thus one is able to image the percept of a particular horse which has been perceived; but he is unable to image correctly the concept of horse as a class or generic term.

In connection with this distinction between perception and conception, we may as well consider the subject of apperception, a term favored by many modern psychologists, although others steadfastly decline to recognize its necessity or meaning and refuse to employ it. Apperception may be defined as: "perception accompanied by comprehension; perception accompanied by recognition." The thing perceived is held to be comprehended or recognized—that is, perceived in a new sense, by reason of certain previously acquired ideas in the mind. Halleck explains it as: "the perception of things in relation to the ideas which we already possess." It follows that all individuals possessed of equally active organs of perception, and equally active attention, will perceive the same thing in the same way and in the same degree. But the apperception of each individual will differ and vary according to his previous experience and training, temperament and taste, habit and custom. For instance, the familiar story of the boy who climbed a tree and watched the passers-by, noting their comments. The first passer-by noticing the tree, says aloud: "That would make a good stick of timber." "Good morning, Mr. Carpenter," said the boy. The next man said: "That tree has fine bark." "Good morning, Mr. Tanner," said the boy. Another said, "I bet there's a squirrel's nest up in that tree." "Good morning, Mr. Hunter," said the boy.

The woman sees in a bird something pretty and "cunning." The hunter sees in it something to kill. The ornithologist sees it as something of a certain genus and species, and perhaps also as something appropriate for his collection. The farmer perceives it to be something destructive of either insects or crops. A thief sees a jail as something to be dreaded; an ordinary citizen, something useful for confining objectionable people; a policeman, something in the line of his business. And so on, the apperception differing upon the previous experience of the individual. In the same way the scientist sees in an animal or rock many qualities of which the ordinary person is ignorant. Our training, experience, prejudices, etc., affect our apperception.

And so, we see that in a measure our concepts are determined not only by our simple perceptions, but also materially by our apperceptions. We conceive things not only as they are apparent to our senses, but also as colored and influenced by our previous impressions and ideas. For this reason we find widely varying concepts of the same things among different individuals. Only an absolute mind could form an absolute concept.

CHAPTER VI.
TERMS

In logic the words concept and term are practically identical, but in the popular usage of the terms there is a distinct difference. This difference is warranted, if we depart from the theoretical phase of logic, for the word concept really denotes an idea in the mind, while the word term really denotes a word or name of an idea or concept—the symbol of the latter. In a previous chapter we have seen that Denomination, or "the act of naming or designating by a name" is the final step or stage in forming a concept. And it is a fact that the majority of the words in the languages of civilized people denote general ideas or concepts. As Brooks says: "To give each individual or particular idea a name peculiar to itself would be impracticable and indeed impossible; the mind would soon become overwhelmed with its burden of names. Nearly all the ordinary words of our language are general rather than particular. The individuals distinguished by particular names, excepting persons and places, are comparatively few. Most objects are named only by common nouns; nearly all of our verbs express general actions; our adjectives denote common qualities, and our adverbs designate classes of actions and qualities. There are very few words in the language, besides the names of persons and places, that do not express general ideas."

In logic the word term is employed to denote any word or words which constitute a concept. The word concept is employed strictly in the sense of a subject of thought, without reference to the words symbolizing it. The concept, or subject of thought, is the important element or fact and the term denoting it is merely a convenient symbol of expression. It must be remembered that a term does not necessarily consists of but a single word, for often many words are employed to denote the concept, sometimes even an entire clause or phrase being found necessary for the current term. For the purpose of the consideration of the subjects to be treated upon in this book, we may agree that: A term is the outward symbol of a concept; and that: The concept is the idea expressed by the term.

There are three general parts or phases of Deductive Logic, namely: Terms, Propositions and Syllogisms. Therefore, in considering Terms we are entering into a consideration of the first phase of Deductive Logic. Unless we have a correct understanding of Terms, we cannot expect to understand the succeeding stages of Deductive Reasoning. As Jevons says: "When we join terms together we make a Proposition; when we join Propositions together, we make an argument or piece of reasoning.... We should generally get nothing but nonsense if we were to put together any terms and any propositions and to suppose that we were reasoning. To produce a good argument we must be careful to obey certain rules, which it is the purpose of Logic to make known. But, in order to understand the matter perfectly, we ought first to learn exactly what a term is, and how many kinds of terms there may be; we have next to learn the nature of a proposition and the different kinds of propositions. Afterwards we shall learn how one proposition may by reasoning be drawn from other propositions in the kind of argument called the syllogism."

Now, having seen that terms are the outward symbols or expression of concepts, and are the names of things which we join together in a proposition, let us proceed to consider the different kinds of terms, following the classifications adopted by the authorities.

A term may contain any number of nouns, substantive or adjective or it may contain but a single noun. Thus in, "Tigers are ferocious," the first term is the single substantive "tigers;" the second term is the single adjective "ferocious." And in the proposition, "The King of England is the Emperor of India," there are two terms, each composed of two nouns, "King of England" being the first term and "Emperor of India" being the second term. The proposition, "The library of the British Museum is the greatest collection of books in the world," contains fifteen words but only two terms; the first term being "The library of the British Museum," in which are two substantives, one adjective, two definite articles and one preposition; the second term being, "the greatest collection of books in the world," which contains three substantives, one adjective, two articles, and two prepositions. The above illustration is supplied by Jevons, who adds: "A logical term, then, may consist of any number of nouns, substantive or adjective, with the articles, prepositions and conjunctions required to join them together; still it is only one term if it points out, or makes us think of a single object, or collection, or class of objects." (A substantive, is: "the part of speech which expresses something that exists, either material or immaterial.")

The first classification of terms divides them into two general classes, viz., (1) Singular Terms; and (2) General Terms.

A Singular Term is a term denoting a single object, person or thing. Although denoting only a single object, person or thing, it may be composed of several words; or it may be composed of but one word as in the case of a proper name, etc. The following are Singular Terms, because they are terms denoting but a single object, person or thing: "Europe; Minnesota; Socrates; Shakespeare; the first man; the highest good; the first cause; the King of England; the British Museum; the Commissioner of Public Works; the main street of the City of New York." It will be noted that in all of the examples given, the Singular Term denotes a particular something, a specific thing, a something of which there is but one, and that one possesses particularity and individuality. As Hyslop says: "Oneness of kind is not the only or distinctive feature of Singular Terms, but individuality, or singularity, as representing a concrete individual whole."

A General Term is a term which applies, in the same sense, to each and every individual object, person or thing in a number of objects, persons or things of the same kind, or to the entire class composed of such objects persons or things of the same kind. For instance, "horse; man; biped; mammal; trees; figures; grain of sand; matter," etc. Hyslop says, regarding General Terms: "In these instances the terms denote more than one object, and apply to all of the same kind. Their meaning is important in the interpretation of what are called universal propositions."

Another general classification of Terms divides them into two respective classes, as follows: (1) Collective Terms; and (2) Distributive Terms. Hyslop says of this classification: "This division is based upon the distinction between aggregate wholes of the same kind and class terms. It partly coincides with the division into Singular and General Terms, the latter always being distributive."

A Collective Term is one which denotes an aggregate or collected whole of objects, persons or things of the same or similar kind, which collective whole is considered as an individual, although composed of a totality of separate individual objects, persons or things. Thus the following terms: "regiment; congregation; army; family; crowd; nation; company; battalion; class; congress; parliament; convention;" etc. are Collective Terms, because they denote collective, aggregate or composite wholes, considered as an individual.

A Distributive Term is a term which denotes each and every individual object, person or thing in a given class. For example, are the terms: "man; quadruped; biped; mammal; book; diamond;

tree." As Hyslop says: "General terms are always distributive." Also: "It is important also to keep clear the distinction between class wholes and collective wholes.... They are often confused so as to call a term denoting a class a Collective Term."

Another general classification of Terms divides them into the following two respective classes; (1) Concrete Terms; and (2) Abstract Terms.

A Concrete Term is a term denoting either a definite object, person or thing which is subject to perception and experience, and may be considered as actually existent concretely, as for instance: horse; man; mountain; dollar; knife; table; etc., or else an attribute thought of and used solely as an attribute, as for instance: "beautiful, wise, noble, virtuous, good," etc.

An Abstract Term is a term denoting the attribute, quality or property considered as apart from the object, person or thing and as having an abstract existence, as for instance: "beauty; wisdom; nobility; goodness; virtue," etc. As we have seen elsewhere, these qualities have no real existence in themselves, but are known and thought of only in connection with concrete objects, persons and things. Thus we cannot know "Beauty," but may know beautiful things; we cannot know "Virtue," but we may know virtuous people, etc.

An attribute or quality is concrete when expressed as an adjective; and abstract when expressed as a noun; as for instance, "beautiful" and "beauty," respectively, or "virtuous" and "virtue," respectively. The distinction may be summed up as follows: A Concrete Term is the name of a thing or of a quality of a thing expressed as an adjective and as merely a quality; while an Abstract Term is the name of a quality of a thing, expressed as a noun and as a "thing" in itself.

Certain terms may be used as either Concrete Terms or as Abstract Terms, and certain authorities have seen fit to classify them as Mixed Terms, as for instance the terms: "government; religion; philosophy;" etc.

Another general classification of Terms divides them into two respective classes as follows: (1) Positive Terms; and (2) Negative Terms.

A Positive Term is a term which denotes its own qualities, as for instance: "good, human, large, square, black, strong," etc. These terms indicate the presence of the quality denoted by the term itself.

A Negative Term is a term denoting the absence of a quality, as for instance: "inhuman, inorganic, unwell, unpleasant, non-conducive," etc. These terms deny the presence of certain qualities, rather than asserting the presence of an opposite quality. They are essentially negative in nature and in form. Jevons says: "We may usually know a Negative Term by its beginning with one of the little syllables un-, in-, a-, an-, non-, or by its ending with -less." Hyslop says: "The usual symbols of Negative Terms are in, un, less, dis, a, or an, anti, mis, and sometimes de, and non and not." Jevons adds: "If the English language were a perfect one, every term ought to have a Negative Term exactly corresponding to it, so that all adjectives and nouns would be in pairs. Just as convenient has its negative inconvenient; metallic, non-metallic; logical, illogical; and so on; so blue should have its negative, non-blue; literary, non-literary; paper, non-paper. But many of these Negative Terms would be seldom or never used, and if we happen to want them, we can make them for the occasion by putting not-, or non-, before the Positive Term. Accordingly, we find in the dictionary only those Negative Terms which are much employed."

The last named authority also says: "Sometimes the same word may seem to have two or even more distinct negatives. There is much difference between undressed and not-dressed, that is 'not in evening dress.' Both seem to be negatives of 'dressed,' but this is because the word has two distinct meanings."

Some authorities insist upon closer and further classification, as for instance, in the case of what they call a Privative Term, denoting the absence of qualities once possessed by the object, person or thing, as: "deaf, dead, blind, dark," etc. Hyslop says that these terms "are Positive in form and Negative in matter or meaning." Also in the case of what they call a Nego-positive Term, denoting "the presence of a positive quality expressed in a negative manner," as: disagreeable, inhuman, invaluable, etc. These last mentioned classes however are regarded by some as the result of "carrying too far" the tendency toward classification, and the two general classes, Positive and Negative, are thought sufficient for the purpose of the general student. The same objection applies to a classification occasionally made i.e., that which is called an Infinitated Term, denoting a term the intent of which is to place in a distinct category every object, person or thing other than that expressed in the corresponding Positive Term. The intent of the term is to place the positive idea in one class, and all else into a separate one. Examples of this class of terms are found in: "not-I, not-animal, not-tree, unmoral," etc. Hyslop says of these terms: "They are not always, if ever, recognized as rhetorically elegant, but are valuable often to make clear the really negative, or infinitatively negative nature of the idea in mind."

Another general classification of Terms divides them into two respective classes, as follows: (1) Absolute Terms; and (2) Relative Terms.

An Absolute Term is a term denoting the presence of qualities intrinsic to the object, and not depending upon any relation to any other object, as for instance: "man; book; horse; gun;" etc. These terms may be related to many other terms, but are not necessarily related to any other.

A Relative Term is a term denoting certain necessary relations to other terms, as for instance: "father; son; mother; daughter; teacher; pupil; master; servant;" etc. Thus it is impossible to think of "child" except in relation to "parent," or vice versa. The one term implies the existence of its related term.

Hyslop says of the above classification: "Relative Terms suggest the thought of other individuals with the relation involved as a part of the term's meaning, while Absolute Terms suggest only the qualities in the subject without a relation to others being necessarily involved."

Some authorities also classify terms as higher and lower; also as broad and narrow. This classification is meant to indicate the content and extent of the term. For instance, when we classify, we begin with the individuals which we then group into a small class. These classes we then group into a larger class, according to their resemblances. These larger classes then go to form a part of still larger classes, and so on. As these classes advance they form broader terms; and as we retreat from the general class into the less general and more particular, the term becomes narrower. By some, the broader term which includes the narrower is called the higher term, and the narrower are called the lower terms. Thus animal would be a higher and broader term than dog, cat or tiger because it includes the latter. Brooks says: "Since a concept is formed by the union of the common attributes of individuals, it thus embraces both attributes and individuals. The attributes of a concept constitute what is called its content; the individuals it embraces constitute its extent."

Accordingly, the feature of including objects in a concept or term is called its extension; while the feature of including attributes or qualities is called its intension. It follows as a natural consequence that the greater the extension of a term, the less its intension; the greater its intension, the less its extension. We will understand this more clearly when we consider that the more individuals contained in a term, the fewer common properties or qualities it can contain; and the more common properties, the fewer individuals. As Brooks says: "The concept man has more extension than poet, orator or statesman, since it embraces more individuals; and less intension, since we must lay aside the distinctive attributes of poet, orator and statesman in order to unite them in a common class man." In the same way the general term animal is quite extended for it includes a large number of individual varieties of very different and varied characteristics and qualities; as for instance, the lion, camel, dog, oyster, elephant, snail, worm, snake, etc. Accordingly its intension must be small for it can include only the qualities common to all animals, which are very few indeed. The definition of the term shows how small is its intension, as: "Animal. An organic being, rising above a vegetable in various respects, especially in possessing sensibility, will and the power of voluntary motion." Another narrows the intension still further when he defines animal as: "a creature which possesses, or has possessed, life." Halleck says: "Animal is very narrow in intension, very broad in extension. There are few qualities common to all animals, but there is a vast number of animals. To give the full meaning of the term in extension, we should have to name every animal, from the microscopic infusoria to the tiger, from the angleworm to the whale. When we decrease the extension to one species of animal, horse, the individuals are fewer, the qualities more numerous."

The importance of forming clear and distinct concepts and of grouping, classifying and generalizing these into larger and broader concepts and terms is recognized by all authorities and is generally regarded as forming the real basis of all constructive thought. As Brooks says: "Generalization lies at the basis of language: only as man can form general conceptions is it possible for him to form a language.... Nearly all the ordinary words in our language are general rather than particular.... This power of generalization lies also at the basis of science. Had we no power of forming general ideas, each particular object would be a study by itself, and we should thus never pass beyond the very alphabet of knowledge. Judgments, except in the simplest form, would be impossible; and it is difficult to see how even the simplest form of the syllogism could be constructed. No general conclusion could be drawn from particulars, nor particular conclusions from generals; and thus neither inductive nor deductive reasoning would be possible. The classifications of science could not be made; and knowledge would end at the very threshold of science."

CHAPTER VII.
THE MEANING OF TERMS

Every term has its meaning, or content, as some authorities prefer to call it. The word or words of which the term is composed are merely vocal sounds, serving as a symbol for the real meaning of the term, which meaning exists only in the mind of the person understanding it. To one not understanding the meaning of the term, the latter is but as a meaningless sound, but to one understanding it the sound awakens mental associations and representation and thus serves its purpose as a symbol of thought.

Each concrete general term has two meanings, (1) the actual concrete thing, person or object to which the term is applied; and (2) the qualities, attributes or properties of those objects, persons or things in consequence of which the term is applied. For instance, in the case of the concrete term book, the first meaning consists of the general idea of the thing which we think of as a book, and the second meaning consists of the various qualities which go to make that thing a book, as the printed pages, the binding, the form, the cover, etc. Not only is that particular thing a book, but every other thing having the same or similar properties also must be a book. And so, whenever I call a thing a book it must possess the said qualities. And, whenever I combine the ideas of these qualities in thought, I must think of a book. As Jevons says: "In reality, every ordinary general term has a double meaning: it means the things to which it is applied, ... it also means, in a totally different way, the qualities and peculiarities implied as being in the things. Logicians say that the number of things to which a term applies is the extension of the term; while the number of qualities or peculiarities implied is the intension."

The extension and intension of terms has been referred to in the previous chapter. The general classification of the degrees of extension of a general term is expressed by the two terms, Genus and Species, respectively. The classification of the character of the intension of a term is expressed by the term, Difference, Property and Accident, respectively.

Genus is a term indicating: "a class of objects containing several species; a class more extensive than a species; a universal which is predicable of several things of different species."

Species is a term denoting: "a smaller class of objects than a genus, and of two or more of which a genus is composed; a predicable that expresses the whole essence of its subject in so far as any common term can express it."

An authority says: "The names species and genus are merely relative and the same common term may, in one case, be the species which is predicated of an individual, and in another case the individual of which a species is predicated. Thus the individual, George, belongs to the logical species Man, while Man is an individual of the logical species Animal." Jevons says: "It is desirable to have names by which to show that one class is contained in another, and accordingly we call the class which is divided into two or more smaller ones, the genus, and the smaller ones into which it is divided, the species." Animal is a genus of which man is a species; while man, in turn, is a genus of which Caucasian is a species; and Caucasian, in turn, becomes a genus of which Socrates becomes a species. The student must avoid confusing the logical meaning of the terms genus and species with the use of the same terms in Natural History. Each class is a "genus" to the class below it in extension; and each class is a "species" to the class above it in extension. At the lowest extreme of the scale we reach what is called the infima species, which cannot be further subdivided, as for instance "Socrates"—this lowest species must always be an individual object, person or thing. At the highest extreme of the scale we reach what is summum genus, or highest genus, which is never a species of anything, for there is no class higher than it, as for instance, "being, existence, reality, truth, the absolute, the infinite, the ultimate," etc. Hyslop says: "In reality there is but one summum genus, while there may be an indefinite number of infimae species. All intermediate terms between these extremes are sometimes called subalterns, as being either genera or species, according to the relation in which they are viewed."

Passing on to the classification of the character of the intension of terms, we find:

Difference, a term denoting: "The mark or marks by which the species is distinguished from the rest of the genus; the specific characteristic." Thus the color of the skin is a difference between the Negro and the Caucasian; the number of feet the difference between the biped and the quadruped; the form and shape of leaves the difference between the oak and the elm trees, etc. Hyslop says: "Whatever distinguishes one object from another can be called the differentia. It is some characteristic in addition to the common qualities and determines the species or individual under the genus."

Property, a term denoting: "A peculiar quality of anything; that which is inherent in or naturally essential to anything." Thus a property is a distinguishing mark of a class. Thus black skin is a property of the Negro race; four feet a property of quadrupeds; a certain form of leaf a property of the oak tree. Thus a difference between two species may be a property of one of the species.

Accident, a term denoting: "Any quality or circumstance which may or may not belong to a class, accidentally as it were; or, whatever does not really constitute an essential part of an object,

43

person or thing." As, for instance, the redness of a rose, for a rose might part with its redness and still be a rose—the color is the accident of the rose. Or, a brick may be white and still be a brick, although the majority of bricks are red—the redness or whiteness of the brick are its accidents and not its essential properties. Whately says: "Accidents in Logic are of two kinds—separable and inseparable. If walking be the accident of a particular man, it is a separable one, for he would not cease to be that man though he stood still; while, on the contrary, if Spaniard is the accident connected with him, it is an inseparable one, since he never can cease to be, ethnologically considered, what he was born."

Arising from the classification of the meaning or content of terms, we find the process termed "Definition."

Definition is a term denoting: "An explanation of a word or term." In Logic the term is used to denote the process of analysis in which the properties and differences of a term are clearly stated. There are of course several kinds of definitions. For instance, there is what is called a Real Definition, which Whately defines as: "A definition which explains the nature of the thing by a particular name." There is also what is called a Physical Definition, which is: "A definition made by enumerating such parts as are actually separable, such as the hull, masts, etc., of a ship." Also a Logical Definition, which is: "A definition consisting of the genus and the difference. Thus if a planet be defined as 'a wandering star,' star is the genus, and wandering points out the difference between a planet and an ordinary star." An Accidental Definition is: "A definition of the accidental qualities of a thing." An Essential Definition is: "a definition of the essential properties and differences of an object, person or thing."

Crabbe discriminates between a Definition and an Explanation, as follows: "A definition is correct or precise; an explanation is general or ample. The definition of a word defines or limits the extent of its signification; it is the rule for the scholar in the use of any word; the explanation of a word may include both definition and illustration; the former admits of no more words than will include the leading features in the meaning of any term; the latter admits of an unlimited scope for diffuseness on the part of the explainer."

Hyslop gives the following excellent explanation of the Logical Definition, which as he states is the proper meaning of the term in Logic. He states:

"The rules which regulate Logical Definition are as follows:

1. A definition should state the essential attributes of the species defined.

2. A definition must not contain the name of word defined. Otherwise the definition is called a circulus in definiendo.

3. The definition must be exactly equivalent to the species defined.

4. A definition should not be expressed in obscure, figurative, or ambiguous language.

5. A definition must not be negative when it can be affirmative."

A correct definition necessarily requires the manifestation of the two respective processes of Analysis and Synthesis.

Analysis is a term denoting: "The separation of anything into its constituent elements, qualities, properties and attributes." It is seen at once that in order to correctly define an object, person or thing, it is first necessary to analyze the latter in order to perceive its essential and accidental properties or differences. Unless the qualities, properties and attributes are clearly and fully perceived, we cannot properly define the object itself.

Synthesis is a term denoting: "The act of joining or putting two or more things together; in Logic: the method by composition, in opposition to the method of resolution or analysis." In stating a definition we must necessarily join together the various essential qualities, properties and attributes, which we have discovered by the process of analysis; and the synthesized combination, considered as a whole, is the definition of the object expressed by the term.

CHAPTER VIII.
JUDGMENTS

The first step in the process of reasoning is that of Conception or the forming of Concepts. The second step is that of Judgment, or the process of perceiving the agreement or disagreement of two conceptions.

Judgment in Logic is defined as: "The comparing together in the mind of two notions, concepts or ideas, which are the objects of apprehension, whether complex or incomplex, and pronouncing that they agree or disagree with each other, or that one of them belongs or does not belong to the other. Judgment is therefore affirmative or negative."

When we have in our mind two concepts, we are likely to compare them one with the other, and to thus arrive at a conclusion regarding their agreement or disagreement. This process of comparison and decision is what, in Logic, is called Judgment.

In every act of Judgment there must be at least two concepts to be examined and compared. This comparison must lead to a Judgment regarding their agreement or disagreement. For instance, we have the two concepts, horse and animal. We examine and compare the two concepts, and find that there is an agreement between them. We find that the concept horse is included in the higher concept of animal and therefore, we assert that: "The horse is an animal." This is a statement of agreement and is, therefore, a Positive Judgment. We then compare the concepts horse and cow and find a disagreement between them, which we express in the statement of the Judgment that: "The horse is not a cow." This Judgment, stating a disagreement is what is called a Negative Judgment.

In the above illustration of the comparison between the concepts horse and animal we find that the second concept animal is broader than the first, horse, so broad in fact that it includes the latter. The terms are not equal, for we cannot say, in truth, that "an animal is the horse." We may, however, include a part of the broader conception with the narrower and say: "some animals are horses." Sometimes both concepts are of equal rank, as when we state that: "Man is a rational animal."

In the process of Judgment there is always the necessity of the choice between the Positive and the Negative. When we compare the concepts horse and animal, we must of necessity decide either that the horse is an animal, or else that it is not an animal.

The importance of the process of Judgment is ably stated by Halleck, as follows: "Were isolated concepts possible, they would be of very little use. Isolated facts are of no more service than unspun wool. We might have a concept of a certain class of three-leaved ivy, as we might also of poisons. Unless judgment linked these two concepts and decided that this species of ivy is poisonous, we might take hold of it and be poisoned. We might have a concept of bread and also one of meat, fruit and vegetables. If we also had a concept of food, unrelated to these, we should starve to death, for we should not think of them as foods. A vessel, supposing itself to be far out at sea, signaled another vessel that the crew were dying of thirst. That crew certainly had a concept of drinkable things and also of water. To the surprise of the first, the second vessel signaled back, 'Draw from the sea and drink. You are at the mouth of the Amazon.' The thirsty crew had not joined the concept drinkable to the concept of water over the ship's side. A man having taken an overdose of laudanum, his wife lost much valuable time in sending out for antidotes, because certain of her concepts had not been connected by judgment. She had good concepts of coffee and of mustard; she also knew that an antidote to opium was needed; but she had never linked these concepts and judged that coffee and mustard were antidotes to opium. The moment she formed that judgment she was a wiser woman for her knowledge was related and usable.... Judgment is the power revolutionizing the world. The revolution is slow because nature's forces are so complex, so hard to be reduced to their simplest forms and so disguised and neutralized by the presence of other forces.... Fortunately judgment is ever silently working and comparing things that, to past ages, have seemed dissimilar; and it is continually abstracting and leaving out of the field of view those qualities which have simply served to obscure the point at issue."

Judgment may be both analytic or synthetic in its processes; and it may be neither. When we compare a narrow concept with a broader one, as a part with a whole, the process is synthetic or an act of combination. When we compare a part of a concept with another concept, the process is analytic. When we compare concepts equal in rank or extent, the process is neither synthetic nor analytic. Thus in the statement that: "A horse is an animal," the judgment is synthetic; in the statement that: "some animals are horses," the judgement is analytic; in the statement that: "a man is a rational animal," the judgment is neither analytic nor synthetic.

Brooks says: "In one sense all judgments are synthetic. A judgment consists of the union of two ideas and this uniting is a process of synthesis. This, however, is a superficial view of the process. Such a synthesis is a mere mechanical synthesis; below this is a thought-process which is sometimes analytic, sometimes synthetic and sometimes neither analytic nor synthetic."

The same authority states: "The act of mind described is what is known as logical judgment. Strictly speaking, however, every intelligent act of the mind is accompanied with a judgment. To know is to discriminate and, therefore, to judge. Every sensation or cognition involves a knowledge and so a judgment that it exists. The mind cannot think at all without judging; to think is to judge. Even in forming the notions which judgment compares, the mind judges. Every notion or concept implies a previous act of judgment to form it: in forming a concept, we compare the common attributes before we unite them; and comparison is judgment. It is thus true that 'Every concept is a contracted judgment; every judgment an expanded concept.' This kind of judgment, by which we affirm the existence of states of consciousness, discriminate qualities, distinguish percepts and form concepts, is called primitive or psychological judgment."

In Logical Judgment there are two aspects; i.e., Judgment by Extension and Judgment by Intension. When we compare the two concepts horse and animal we find that the concept horse is contained in the concept animal and the judgment that "a horse is an animal" may be considered as a Judgment by Extension. In the same comparison we see that the concept horse contains the quality of animality, and in attributing this quality to the horse, we may also say "the horse is an animal," which judgment may be considered as a Judgment by Intension. Brooks says: "Both views of Judgment are correct; the mind may reach its judgment either by extension or by intension. The method by extension is usually the more natural."

When a Judgment is expressed in words it is called a Proposition. There is some confusion regarding the two terms, some holding that a Judgment and a proposition are identical, and that the term "proposition" may be properly used to indicate the judgment itself. But the authorities who seek for clearness of expression and thought now generally hold that: "A Proposition is a Judgment expressed in words." In the next chapter, in which we consider

Propositions, we shall enter into a more extended consideration of the subject of Judgments as expressed in Propositions, which consideration we omit at this point in order to avoid repetition. Just as the respective subjects of Concepts and Terms necessarily blend into each other, so do the respective subjects of Judgments and Propositions. In each case, too, there is the element of the mental process on the one hand and the verbal expression of it on the other hand. It will be well to keep this fact in mind.

CHAPTER IX.
PROPOSITIONS

We have seen that the first step of Deductive Reasoning is that which we call Concepts. The second step is that which we call Propositions.

In Logic, a Proposition is: "A sentence, or part of a sentence, affirming or denying a connection between the terms; limited to express assertions rather than extended to questions and commands." Hyslop defines a Proposition as: "any affirmation or denial of an agreement between two conceptions."

Examples of Propositions are found in the following sentences: "The rose is a flower;" "a horse is an animal;" "Chicago is a city;" all of which are affirmations of agreement between the two terms involved; also in: "A horse is not a zebra;" "pinks are not roses;" "the whale is not a fish;" etc., which are denials of agreement between the terms.

The Parts of a Proposition are: (1) the Subject, or that of which something is affirmed or denied; (2) the Predicate, or the something which is affirmed or denied regarding the Subject; and (3) the Copula, or the verb serving as a link between the Subject and the Predicate.

In the Proposition: "Man is an animal," the term man is the Subject; the term an animal is the Predicate; and the word is, is the Copula. The Copula is always some form of the verb to be, in the present tense indicative, in an affirmative Proposition; and the same with the negative particle affixed, in a negative Proposition. The Copula is not always directly expressed by the word is or is not, etc., but is instead expressed in some phrase which implies them. For instance, we say "he runs," which implies "he is running." In the same way, it may appear at times as if the Predicate was missing, as in: "God is," by which is meant "God is existing." In some cases, the Proposition is inverted, the Predicate appearing first in order, and the Subject last, as in: "Blessed are the peacemakers;" or "Strong is Truth." In such cases judgment must be used in determining the matter, in accordance with the character and meaning of the terms.

An Affirmative Proposition is one in which the Predicate is affirmed to agree with the Subject. A Negative Proposition is one in which the agreement of the Predicate and Subject is denied. Examples of both of these classes have been given in this chapter.

Another classification of Propositions divides them in three classes, as follows (1) Categorical; (2) Hypothetical; (3) Disjunctive.

A Categorical Proposition is one in which the affirmation or denial is made without reservation or qualification, as for instance: "Man is an animal;" "the rose is a flower," etc. The fact asserted may not be true, but the statement is made positively as a statement of reality.

A Hypothetical Proposition is one in which the affirmation or denial is made to depend upon certain conditions, circumstances or suppositions, as for instance: "If the water is boiling-hot, it will scald;" or "if the powder be damp, it will not explode," etc. Jevons says: "Hypothetical Propositions may generally be recognized by containing the little word 'if;' but it is doubtful whether they really differ much from the ordinary propositions.... We may easily say that 'boiling water will scald,' and 'damp gunpowder will not explode,' thus avoiding the use of the word 'if.'"

A Disjunctive Proposition is one "implying or asserting an alternative," and usually containing the conjunction "or," sometimes together with "either," as for instance: "Lightning is sheet or forked;" "Arches are either round or pointed;" "Angles are either obtuse, right angled or acute."

Another classification of Propositions divides them in two classes as follows: (1) Universal; (2) Particular.

A Universal Proposition is one in which the whole quantity of the Subject is involved in the assertion or denial of the Predicate. For instance: "All men are liars," by which is affirmed that all of the entire race of men are in the category of liars, not some men but all the men that are in existence. In the same way the Proposition: "No men are immortal" is Universal, for it is a universal denial.

A Particular Proposition is one in which the affirmation or denial of the Predicate involves only a part or portion of the whole of the Subject, as for instance: "Some men are atheists," or "Some women are not vain," in which cases the affirmation or denial does not involve all or the whole of the Subject. Other examples are: "A few men," etc.; "many people," etc.; "certain books," etc.; "most people," etc.

Hyslop says: "The signs of the Universal Proposition, when formally expressed, are all, every, each, any, and whole or words with equivalent import." The signs of Particular Propositions are also certain adjectives of quantity, such as some, certain, a few, many, most or such others as denote at least a part of a class.

The subject of the Distribution of Terms in Propositions is considered very important by Logicians, and as Hyslop says: "has much importance in determining the legitimacy, or at least the intelligibility, of our reasoning and the assurance that it will be accepted by others." Some authorities favor the term, "Qualification of the Terms of Propositions," but the established usage favors the term "Distribution."

The definition of the Logical term, "Distribution," is: "The distinguishing of a universal whole into its several kinds of species; the employment of a term to its fullest extent; the application of a term to its fullest extent, so as to include all significations or applications." A Term of a Proposition is distributed when it is employed in its fullest sense; that is to say, when it is employed so as to apply to each and every object, person or thing included under it. Thus in the proposition, "All horses are animals," the term horses is distributed; and in the proposition, "Some horses are thoroughbreds," the term horses is not distributed. Both of these examples relate to the distribution of the subject of the proposition. But the predicate of a proposition also may or may not be distributed. For instance, in the proposition, "All horses are animals," the predicate, animals, is not distributed, that is, not used in its fullest sense, for all animals are not horses—there are some animals which are not horses and, therefore, the predicate, animals, not being used in its fullest sense is said to be "not distributed." The proposition really means: "All horses are some animals."

There is however another point to be remembered in the consideration of Distribution of Terms of Propositions, which Brooks expresses as follows: "Distribution generally shows itself in the form of the expression, but sometimes it may be determined by the thought. Thus if we say, 'Men are mortal,' we mean all men, and the term men is distributed. But if we say 'Books are necessary to a library,' we mean, not 'all books' but 'some books.' The test of distribution is whether the term applies to 'each and every.' Thus when we say 'men are mortal,' it is true of each and every man that he is mortal."

The Rules of Distribution of the Terms of Proposition are as follows:

1. All universals distribute the subject.

2. All particulars do not distribute the subject.

3. All negatives distribute the predicate.

4. All affirmatives do not distribute the predicate.

The above rules are based upon logical reasoning. The reason for the first two rules is quite obvious, for when the subject is universal, it follows that the whole subject is involved; when the subject is particular it follows that only a part of the subject is involved. In the case of the third rule, it will be seen that in every negative proposition the whole of the predicate must be denied the subject, as for instance, when we say: "Some animals are not horses," the whole class of horses is cut off from the subject, and is thus distributed. In the case of the fourth rule, we may readily see that in the affirmative proposition the whole of the predicate is not denied the subject, as for instance, when we say that: "Horses are animals," we do not mean that horses are all the animals, but that they are merely a part or portion of the class animal—therefore, the predicate, animals, is not distributed.

In addition to the forms of Propositions given there is another class of Propositions known as Definitive or Substitutive Propositions, in which the Subject and the Predicate are exactly alike in extent and rank. For instance, in the proposition, "A triangle is a polygon of three sides" the two terms are interchangeable; that is, may be substituted for each other. Hence the term "substitutive." The term "definitive" arises from the fact that the respective terms of this kind of a proposition necessarily define each other. All logical definitions are expressed in this last mentioned form of proposition, for in such cases the subject and the predicate are precisely equal to each other.

CHAPTER X.
IMMEDIATE REASONING

In the process of Judgment we must compare two concepts and ascertain their agreement of disagreement. In the process of Reasoning we follow a similar method and compare two judgments, the result of such comparison being the deduction of a third judgment.

The simplest form of reasoning is that known as Immediate Reasoning, by which is meant the deduction of one proposition from another which implies it. Some have defined it as: "reasoning without a middle term." In this form of reasoning only one proposition is required for the premise, and from that premise the conclusion is deduced directly and without the necessity of comparison with any other term of proposition.

The two principal methods employed in this form of Reasoning are; (1) Opposition; (2) Conversion.

Opposition exists between propositions having the same subject and predicate, but differing in quality or quantity, or both. The Laws of Opposition are as follows:

I. (1) If the universal is true, the particular is true. (2) If the particular is false, the universal is false. (3) If the universal is false, nothing follows. (4) If the particular is true, nothing follows.

II. (1) If one of two contraries is true, the other is false. (2) If one of two contraries is false, nothing can be inferred. (3) Contraries are never both true, but both may be false.

III. (1) If one of two sub-contraries is false, the other is true. (2) If one of two sub-contraries is true, nothing can be inferred concerning the other. (3) Sub-contraries can never be both false, but both may be true.

IV. (1) If one of two contradictories is true, the other is false. (2) If one of two contradictories is false, the other is true. (3) Contradictories can never be both true or both false, but always one is true and the other is false.

In order to comprehend the above laws, the student should familiarize himself with the following arrangement, adopted by logicians as a convenience:

We start with Propostions on the left, then across the top we next have Universal and then Affirmative (A) and Negative (E).

Now back to Propositions on the left, then across the bottom we next have Particular and then Affirmative (I) and Negative (O).

Examples of the above: Universal Affirmative (A): "All men are mortal;" Universal Negative (E): "No man is mortal;" Particular Affirmative (I): "Some men are mortal;" Particular Negative (O): "Some men are not mortal."

The following examples of abstract propositions are often used by logicians as tending toward a clearer conception than examples such as given above:

(A) "All A is B."

(I) "Some A is B."

(E) "No A is B."

(O) "Some A is not B."

These four forms of propositions bear certain logical relations to each other, as follows:

A and E are styled contraries. I and O are sub-contraries; A and I and also E and O are called subalterns; A and O and also I and E are styled contradictories.

A close study of these relations, and the symbols expressing them, is necessary for a clear comprehension of the Laws of Opposition stated a little further back, as well as the principles of Conversion which we shall mention a little further on. The following chart, called the Square of Opposition, is also employed by logicians to illustrate the relations between the four classes of propositions:

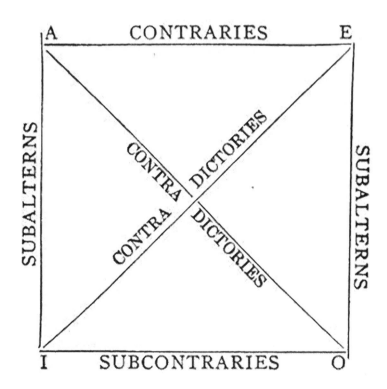

Conversion is the process of immediate reasoning by which we infer from a given proposition another proposition having the predicate of the original for its subject and the subject of the original for its predicate; or stated in a few words: Conversion is the transposition of the subject and predicate of a proposition. As Brooks states it: "Propositions or judgments are converted when the subject and predicate change places in such a manner that the resulting judgment is an inference from the given judgment." The new proposition, resulting from the operation or Conversion, is called the Converse; the original proposition is called the Convertend.

The Law of Conversion is that: "No term must be distributed in the Converse that is not distributed in the Convertend." This arises from the obvious fact that nothing should be affirmed in the derived proposition than there is in the original proposition.

There are three kinds of Conversion; viz: (1) Simple Conversion; (2) Conversion by Limitation; (3) Conversion by Contraposition.

In Simple Conversion there is no change in either quality or quantity. In Conversion by Limitation the quality is changed from universal to particular. In Conversion by Negation the quality is changed but not the quantity. Referring to the classification tables and symbols given in the preceding pages of this chapter, we may now proceed to consider the application of these methods of Conversion to each of the four kinds of propositions; as follows:

The Universal Affirmative (symbol A) proposition is converted by Limitation, or by a change of quality from universal to particular. The predicate not being "distributed" in the convertend, we must not distribute it in the converse by saying "all." Thus in this case we must convert the proposition, "all men are mortal" (A), into "some mortals are men" (I).

The Universal Negative (symbol E) is converted by Simple Conversion, in which there is no change in either quality or quantity. For since both terms of "E" are distributed, they may both be distributed in the converse without violating the law of conversion. Thus "No man is mortal" is converted into: "No mortals are men." "E" is converted into "E."

The Particular Affirmative (symbol I) is also converted by Simple Conversion in which there is no change in either quality or quantity. For since neither term is distributed in "I," neither term may be distributed in the converse, and the latter must remain "I." For instance; the proposition: "Some men are mortal" is converted into the proposition, "Some mortals are men."

The Particular Negative (symbol O) is converted by Conversion by Negation, in which the quality is changed but not the quantity. Thus in converting the proposition: "Some men are not mortal," we must not say "some mortals are not men," for in so doing we would distribute men in the predicate, where it is not distributed in the convertend. Avoiding this, we transfer the negative particle from the copula to the predicate so that the convertend becomes "I" which is converted by Simple Conversion. Thus we transfer "Some men are not mortal" into "Some men are not-mortal" from which we easily convert (by simple Conversion) the proposition: "Some not-mortals are men."

It will be well for students, at this point, to consider the three following Fundamental Laws of Thought as laid down by the authorities, which are as follows:

The Law of Identity, which states that: "The same quality or thing is always the same quality or thing, no matter how different the conditions in which it occurs."

The Law of Contradiction, which states that: "No thing can at the same time and place both be and not be."

The Law of Excluded Middle, which states that: "Everything must either be or not be; there is no other alternative or middle course."

Of these laws, Prof. Jevons, a noted authority, says: "Students are seldom able to see at first their full meaning and importance. All arguments may be explained when these self-evident laws are granted; and it is not too much to say that the whole of logic will be plain to those who will constantly use these laws as the key."

CHAPTER XI.
INDUCTIVE REASONING

Inductive Reasoning, as we have said, is the process of discovering general truth from particular truths, or inferring general laws from particular facts. Thus, from the experience of the individual and the race regarding the particular truth that each and every man under observation has been observed to die sooner or later, it is inferred that all men die, and hence, the induction of the general truth that "All men must die." Or, as from experience we know that the various kinds of metals expand when subjected to heat, we infer that all metals are subject to this law, and that consequently we may arrive by inductive reasoning at the conclusion that: "All metals expand when subjected to heat." It will be noticed that the conclusion arrived at in this way by Inductive Reasoning forms the fundamental premise in the process of Deductive Reasoning. As we have seen elsewhere, the two processes, Inductive and Deductive Reasoning, respectively are interdependent—resting upon one another.

Jevons says of Inductive Reasoning: "In Deductive Reasoning we inquire how we may gather the truth contained in some propositions called Premises, and put into another proposition called the Conclusion. We have not yet undertaken to find out how we can learn what propositions really are true, but only what propositions are true when other ones are true. All the acts of reasoning yet considered would be called deductive because we deduce, or lead down the truth from premises to conclusion. It is an exceedingly important thing to understand deductive inference correctly, but it might seem to be still more important to understand inductive inference, by which we gather the truth of general propositions from facts observed as happening in the world around us." Halleck says: "Man has to find out through his own experience, or that of others, the major premises from which he argues or draws his conclusions. By induction we examine what seems to us a sufficient number of individual cases. We then conclude that the rest of these cases, which we have not examined, will obey the same general law.... Only after general laws have been laid down, after objects have been classified, after major premises have been formed, can deduction be employed."

Strange as may now appear, it is a fact that until a comparatively recent period in the history of man, it was held by philosophers that the only way to arrive at all knowledge was by means of Deductive Reasoning, by the use of the Syllogism. The influence of Aristotle was great and men preferred to pursue artificial and complicated methods of Deductive Reasoning, rather than to reach the truth by obtaining the facts from Nature herself, at first hand, and then inferring general principle from the facts so gathered. The rise of modern scientific methods of reasoning, along the lines of Inductive Inference, dates from about 1225-1300. Roger Bacon was one of the first to teach that we must arrive at scientific truth by a process of observation and experimentation on the natural objects to be found on all sides. He made many discoveries by following this process. He was ably seconded by Galileo who lived some three hundred years later, and who also taught that many great general truths might be gained by careful observation and intelligent inference. Lord Francis Bacon, who lived about the same time as Galileo, presented in his Novum Organum many excellent observations and facts regarding the process of Inductive Reasoning and scientific thought. As Jevons says: "Inductive logic inquires by what manner of reasoning we can gather the laws of nature from the facts and events observed. Such reasoning is called induction, or inductive inquiry, and, as it has actually been practiced by all the great discoverers in science, it consists in four steps."

The Four Steps in Inductive Reasoning, as stated by Jevons, are as follows:

First Step.—Preliminary observation.

Second Step.—The making of hypotheses.

Third Step.—Deductive reasoning.

Fourth Step.—Verification.

It will be seen that the process of Inductive Reasoning is essentially a synthetic process, because it operates in the direction of combining and uniting particular facts or truths into general truths or laws which comprehend, embrace and include them all. As Brooks says: "The particular facts are united by the mind into the general law; the general law embraces the particular facts and binds them together into a unity of principle and thought. Induction is thus a process of thought from the parts to the whole—a synthetic process." It will also be seen that the process of Inductive Reasoning is essentially an ascending process, because it ascends from particular facts to general laws; particular truths to universal truths; from the lower to the higher, the narrower to the broader, the smaller to the greater.

Brooks says of Inductive Reasoning: "The relation of induction to deduction will be clearly seen. Induction and Deduction are the converse, the opposites of each other. Deduction derives a particular truth from a general truth; Induction derives a general truth from particular truths. This antithesis appears in every particular. Deduction goes from generals to particulars; Induction goes from particulars to generals. Deduction is an analytic process; Induction is a synthetic process. Deduction is a descending process—it goes from the higher truth to the lower truth; Induction is an ascending process—it goes from the lower truth to the higher. They differ also in that Deduction may be applied to necessary truths, while Induction is mainly restricted to contingent truths." Hyslop says: "There have been several ways of defining this process. It has been usual to contrast it with Deduction. Now, deduction is often said to be reasoning from general to particular truths, from the containing to the contained truth, or from cause to effect. Induction, therefore, by contrast is defined as reasoning from the particular to the general, from the contained to the containing, or from effect to cause. Sometimes induction is said to be reasoning from the known to the unknown. This would make deduction, by contrast, reasoning from the unknown to the known, which is absurd. The former ways of representing it are much the better. But there is still a better way of comparing them. Deduction is reasoning in which the conclusion is contained in the premises. This is a ground for its certitude and we commit a fallacy whenever we go beyond the premises as shown by the laws of the distribution of terms. In contrast with this, then, we may call inductive reasoning the process by which we go beyond the premises in the conclusion.... The process here is to start from given facts and to infer some other probable facts more general or connected with them. In this we see the process of going beyond the premises. There are, of course, certain conditions which regulate the legitimacy of the procedure, just as there are conditions determining deduction. They are that the conclusion shall represent the same general kind as the premises, with a possibility of accidental differences. But it goes beyond the premises in so far as known facts are concerned."

The following example may give you a clearer idea of the processes of Inductive Reasoning:

First Step. Preliminary Observation. Example: We notice that all the particular magnets which have come under our observation attract iron. Our mental record of the phenomena may be stated as: "A, B, C, D, E, F, G, etc., and also X, Y, and Z, all of which are magnets, in all observed instances, and at all observed times, attract iron."

Second Step. The Making of Hypotheses. Example: Upon the basis of the observations and experiments, as above stated, and applying the axiom of Inductive Reasoning, that: "What is true of the many, is true of the whole," we feel justified in forming a hypothesis or inference of a general law or truth, applying the facts of the particulars to the general, whole or universal, thus: "All magnets attract iron."

Third Step. Deductive Reasoning. Example: Picking up a magnet regarding which we have had no experience and upon which we have made no experiments, we reason by the syllogism, as follows: (1) All magnets attract iron; (2) This thing is a magnet; therefore (3) This thing will attract iron. In this we apply the axiom of Deductive Reasoning: "Whatever is true of the whole is true of the parts."

Fourth Step. Verification. Example: We then proceed to test the hypothesis upon the particular magnet, so as to ascertain whether or not it agrees with the particular facts. If the magnet does not attract iron we know that either our hypothesis is wrong and that some magnets do not attract iron; or else that our judgment regarding that particular "thing" being a magnet is at fault and that it is not a magnet. In either case, further examination, observation and experiment is necessary. In case the particular magnet does attract iron, we feel that we have verified our hypothesis and our judgment.

CHAPTER XII.
REASONING BY INDUCTION

The term "Induction," in its logical usage, is defined as follows: "(a) The process of investigating and collecting facts; and (b) the deducing of an inference from these facts; also (c) sometimes loosely used in the sense of an inference from observed facts." Mill says: "Induction, then, is that operation of the mind, by which we infer that what we know to be true in a particular case or cases, will be true in all cases which resemble the former in certain assignable respects. In other words, Induction is the process by which we conclude that what is true of certain individuals of a class, is true of the whole class, or that what is true at certain times will be true in similar circumstances at all times."

The Basis of Induction is the axiom that: "What is true of the many is true of the whole." Esser, a well known authority, states this axiom in rather more complicated form, as follows: "That which belongs or does not belong to many things of the same kind, belongs or does not belong to all things of the same kind."

This basic axiom of Induction rests upon the conviction that Nature's laws and manifestations are regular, orderly and uniform. If we assume that Nature does not manifest these qualities, then the axiom must fall, and all inductive reason must be fallacious. As Brooks well says: "Induction has been compared to a ladder upon which we ascend from facts to laws. This ladder cannot stand unless it has something to rest upon; and this something is our faith in the constancy of Nature's laws." Some authorities have held that this perception of the uniformity of Nature's laws is in the nature of an intuitive truth, or an inherent law of our intelligence. Others hold that it is in itself an inductive truth, arrived at by experience and observation at a very early age. We are held to have noticed the uniformity in natural phenomena, and almost instinctively infer that this uniformity is continuous and universal.

The authorities assume the existence of two kinds of Induction, namely: (1) Perfect Induction; and (2) Imperfect Induction. Other, but similar, terms are employed by different authorities to designate these two classes.

Perfect Induction necessitates a knowledge of all the particulars forming a class; that is, all the individual objects, persons, things or facts comprising a class must be known and enumerated in this form of Induction. For instance, if we knew positively all of Brown's children, and that their names were John, Peter, Mark, Luke, Charles, William, Mary and Susan, respectively; and that each and every one of them were freckled and had red hair; then, in that case, instead of simply generalizing and stating that: "John, Peter, Mark, Luke, Charles, William, Mary and Susan, who are all of Brown's children, are freckled and have red hair," we would save words, and state the inductive conclusion: "All Brown's children are freckled and have red hair." It will be noticed that in this case we include in the process only what is stated in the premise itself, and we do not extend our inductive process beyond the actual data upon which it is based. This form of Induction is sometimes called "Logical Induction," because the inference is a logical necessity, without the possibility of error or exception. By some authorities it is held not to be Induction at all, in the strict sense, but little more than a simplified form of enumeration. In actual practice it is seldom available, for it is almost impossible for us to know all the particulars in inferring a general law or truth. In view of this difficulty, we fall back upon the more practical form of induction known as:

Imperfect Induction, or as it is sometimes called "Practical Induction," by which is meant the inductive process of reasoning in which we assume that the particulars or facts actually known to us correctly represent those which are not actually known, and hence the whole class to which they belong. In this process it will be seen that the conclusion extends beyond the data upon which it is based. In this form of Induction we must actually employ the principle of the axiom: "What is true of the many is true of the whole"—that is, must assume it to be a fact, not because we know it by actual experience, but because we infer it from the axiom which also agrees with past experience. The conclusion arrived at may not always be true in its fullest sense, as in the case of the conclusion of Perfect Induction, but is the result of an inference based upon a principle which gives us a reasonable right to assume its truth in absence of better knowledge.

In considering the actual steps in the process of Inductive Reasoning we can do no better than to follow the classification of Jevons, mentioned in the preceding chapter, the same being simple and readily comprehended, and therefore preferable in this case to the more technical classification favored by some other authorities. Let us now consider these four steps.

First Step. Preliminary observation. It follows that without the experience of oneself or of others in the direction of observing and remembering particular facts, objects, persons and things, we cannot hope to acquire the preliminary facts for the generalization and inductive inference necessary in Inductive Reasoning. It is necessary for us to form a variety of clear Concepts or ideas of facts, objects, persons and things, before we may hope to generalize from these particulars. In the chapters of this book devoted to the consideration of Concepts, we may see the fundamental importance of the formation and acquirement of correct Concepts. Concepts are the fundamental material for correct reasoning. In order to produce a perfect finished product, we must have perfect materials, and a sufficient quantity of them. The greater the knowledge one possesses of the facts and objects of the outside world, the better able is he to reason therefrom. Concepts are the raw material which must feed the machinery of reasoning, and from which the final product of perfected thought is produced. As Halleck says: "There must first be a presentation of materials. Suppose that we wish to form the concept fruit. We must first perceive the different kinds of fruit—cherry, pear, quince, plum, currant, apple, fig, orange, etc. Before we can take the next step, we must be able to form distinct and accurate images of the various kinds of fruit. If the concept is to be absolutely accurate, not one kind of fruit must be overlooked. Practically this is impossible; but many kinds should be examined. Where perception is inaccurate and stinted, the products of thought cannot be trustworthy. No building is firm if reared on insecure foundations."

In the process of Preliminary Observation, we find that there are two ways of obtaining a knowledge of the facts and things around us. These two ways are as follows:

I. By Simple Observation, or the perception of the happenings which are manifested without our interference. In this way we perceive the motion of the tides; the movement of the planets; the phenomena of the weather; the passing of animals, etc.

II. By the Observation of Experiment, or the perception of happenings in which we interfere with things and then observe the result. An experiment is: "A trial, proof, or test of anything; an act, operation, or process designed to discover some unknown truth, principle or effect, or to test some received or reputed truth or principle." Hobbes says: "To have had many experiments is what we call experience." Jevons says: "Experimentation is observation with something more; namely, regulation of the things whose behavior is to be observed. The advantages of experiment over mere observation are of two kinds. In the first place, we shall generally know much more certainly and accurately with what we are dealing, when we make experiments than when we simply observe natural events.... It is a further advantage of artificial experiments, that they enable us to discover entirely new substances and to learn their properties.... It would be a mistake to suppose that the making of an experiment is inductive reasoning, and gives us without further trouble the laws of nature. Experiments only give us the facts upon which we may afterward reason.... Experiments then merely give facts, and it is only by careful reasoning that we can learn when the same facts will be observed again. The general rule is that the same causes will produce the same effects. Whatever happens in one case will happen in all like cases, provided that they are really like, and not merely apparently so.... When we have by repeated experiments tried the effect which all the surrounding things might have on the result, we can then reason with much confidence as to similar results in similar circumstances.... In order that we may, from our observations and experiments, learn the law of nature and become able to foresee the future, we must perform the process of generalization. To generalize is to draw a general law from particular cases, and to infer that what we see to be true of a few things is true of the whole genus or class to which these things belong. It requires much judgment and skill to generalize correctly, because everything depends upon the number and character of the instances about which we reason."

Having seen that the first step in Inductive Reasoning is Preliminary Observation, let us now consider the next steps in which we may see what we do with the facts and ideas which we have acquired by this Observation and Experiment.

CHAPTER XIII.
THEORY AND HYPOTHESES

Following Jevons' classification, we find that the Second Step in Inductive Reasoning is that called "The Making of Hypotheses."

A Hypothesis is: "A supposition, proposition or principle assumed or taken for granted in order to draw a conclusion or inference in proof of the point or question; a proposition assumed or taken for granted, though not proved, for the purpose of deducing proof of a point in question." It will be seen that a Hypothesis is merely held to be possibly or probably true, and not certainly true; it is in the nature of a working assumption, whose truth must be tested by observed facts. The assumption may apply either to the cause of things, or to the laws which govern things. Akin to a hypothesis, and by many people confused in meaning with the latter, is what is called a Theory.

A Theory is: "A verified hypothesis; a hypothesis which has been established as, apparently, the true one." An authority says "Theory is a stronger word than hypothesis. A theory is founded on principles which have been established on independent evidence. A hypothesis merely assumes the operation of a cause which would account for the phenomena, but has not evidence that such cause was actually at work. Metaphysically, a theory is nothing but a hypothesis supported by a large amount of probable evidence." Brooks says: "When a hypothesis is shown to explain all the facts that are known, these facts being varied and extensive, it is said to be verified, and becomes a theory. Thus we have the theory of universal gravitation, the Copernican theory of the solar system, the undulatory theory of light, etc., all of which were originally mere hypotheses. This is the manner in which the term is usually employed in the inductive philosophy; though it must be admitted that it is not always used in this strict sense. Discarded hypotheses are often referred to as theories; and that which is actually a theory is sometimes called a hypothesis."

The steps by which we build up a hypothesis are numerous and varied. In the first place we may erect a hypothesis by the methods of what we have described as Perfect Induction, or Logical Induction. In this case we proceed by simple generalization or simple enumeration. The example of the freckled, red-haired children of Brown, mentioned in a previous chapter, explains this method. It requires the examination and knowledge of every object or fact of which the statement or hypothesis is made. Hamilton states that it is the only induction which is absolutely necessitated by the laws of thought. It does not extend further than the plane of experience. It is akin to mathematical reasoning.

Far more important is the process by which hypotheses are erected by means of inferences from Imperfect Induction, by which we reason from the known to the unknown, transcending experience, and making true inductive inferences from the axiom of Inductive Reasoning. This process involves the subject of Causes. Jevons says: "The cause of an event is that antecedent, or set of antecedents, from which the event always follows. People often make much difficulty about understanding what the cause of an event means, but it really means nothing beyond the things that must exist before in order that the event shall happen afterward."

Causes are often obscure and difficult to determine. The following five difficulties are likely to arise: I. The cause may be out of our experience, and is therefore not to be understood; II. Causes often act conjointly, so that it is difficult to discover the one predominant cause by reason of its associated causes; III. Often the presence of a counteracting, or modifying cause may confuse us; IV. Often a certain effect may be caused by either of several possible causes; V. That which appears as a cause of a certain effect may be but a co-effect of an original cause.

Mill formulated several tests for ascertaining the causal agency in particular cases, in view of the above-stated difficulties. These tests are as follows: (1) The Method of Agreement; (2) The Method of Difference; (3) The Method of Residues; and (4) The Method of Concomitant Variations. The following definitions of these various tests are given by Atwater as follows:

Method of Agreement: "If, whenever a given object or agency is present without counteracting forces, a given effect is produced, there is a strong evidence that the object or agency is the cause of the effect."

Method of Difference: "If, when the supposed cause is present the effect is present, and when the supposed cause is absent the effect is wanting, there being in neither case any other agents present to effect the result, we may reasonably infer that the supposed cause is the real one."

Method of Residue: "When in any phenomena we find a result remaining after the effects of all known causes are estimated, we may attribute it to a residual agent not yet reckoned."

Method of Concomitant Variations: "When a variation in a given antecedent is accompanied by a variation of a given consequent, they are in some manner related as cause and effect."

Atwater adds: "Whenever either of these criteria is found free from conflicting evidence, and especially when several of them concur, the evidence is clear that the cases observed are fair representatives of the whole class, and warrant a valid inductive conclusion."

Jevons gives us the following valuable rules:

I. "Whenever we can alter the quantity of the things experimented on, we can apply a rule for discovering which are causes and which are effects, as follows: We must vary the quantity of one thing, making it at one time greater and at another time less, and if we observe any other thing which varies just at the same times, it will in all probability be an effect."

II. "When things vary regularly and frequently, there is a simple rule, by following which we can judge whether changes are connected together as causes and effects, as follows: Those things which change in exactly equal times are in all likelihood connected together."

III. "It is very difficult to explain how it is that we can ever reason from one thing to a class of things by generalization, when we cannot be sure that the things resemble each other in the important points.... Upon what grounds do we argue? We have to get a general law from particular facts. This can only be done by going through all the steps of inductive reasoning. Having made certain observations, we must frame hypotheses as to the circumstances, or laws from which they proceed. Then we must reason deductively; and after verifying the deductions in as many cases as possible, we shall know how far we can trust similar deductions concerning future events.... It is difficult to judge when we may, and when we may not, safely infer from some things to others in this simple way, without making a complete theory of the matter. The only rule that can be given to assist us is that if things resemble each other in a few properties only, we must observe many instances before inferring that these properties will always be joined together in other cases."

CHAPTER XIV.
MAKING AND TESTING HYPOTHESES

The older philosophers and logicians were often at a loss how to reasonably account for the origin of hypotheses. It will be seen, after giving the matter a little thought, that the actual formation of the hypothesis is more than a mere grouping together or synthesis of facts or ideas—there is another mental process which actually evolves the hypothesis or theory—which gives a possible reason. What is this mental process? Let us consider the matter. Brooks well says: "The hypotheses of science originate in what is called anticipation. They are not the result of a mere synthesis of facts, for no combination of facts can give the law or cause. We do not see the law; we see the facts and the mind thinks the law. By the power of anticipation, the mind often leaps from a few facts to the cause which produces them or the law which governs them. Many hypotheses were but a happy intuition of the mind. They were the result of what La Place calls 'a great guess,' or what Plato so beautifully designates as 'a sacred suspicion of truth.' The forming of hypotheses requires a suggestive mind, a lively fancy, a philosophic imagination, that catches a glimpse of the idea through the form, or sees the law standing behind the fact."

The student of The New Psychology sees in the mental operation of the forming of the hypothesis—"the mind thinking the law"—but an instance of the operation of the activities of the Subconscious Mind, or even the Superconscious Mind. (See the volume on the Subconscious Mind in this series.) Not only does this hypothesis give the explanation which the old psychology has failed to do, but it agrees with the ideas of others on the subject as stated in the above quotation from Brooks; and moreover agrees with many recorded instances of the formation of great hypotheses. Sir Wm. Hamilton discovered the very important mathematical law of quaternions while walking one day in the

Dublin Observatory. He had pondered long on the subject, but without result. But, finally, on that eventful day he suddenly "felt the galvanic circle of thought" close, and the result was the realization of the fundamental mathematical relations of the problem. Berthelot, the founder of Synthetic Chemistry, has testified that the celebrated experiments which led to his remarkable discoveries were seldom the result of carefully followed lines of conscious thought or pure reasoning processes; but, instead, came to him "of their own accord," so to speak, "as from a clear sky." In these and many other similar instances, the mental operation was undoubtedly purely subjective and subconscious. Dr. Hudson has claimed that the "Subjective Mind" cannot reason inductively, and that its operations are purely and distinctly deductive, but the testimony of many eminent scientists, inventors and philosophers is directly to the contrary.

In this connection the following quotation from Thomson is interesting: "The system of anatomy which has immortalized the name of Oken is the consequence of a flash of anticipation which glanced through his mind when he picked up in a chance walk the skull of a deer, bleached and disintegrated by the weather, and exclaimed after a glance, 'It is part of a vertebral column!' When Newton saw the apple fall, the anticipatory question flashed through his mind, 'Why do not the heavenly bodies fall like this apple?' In neither case had accident any important share; Newton and Oken were prepared by the deepest previous study to seize upon the unimportant fact offered to them, and to show how important it might become; and if the apple and the deer-skull had been wanting, some other falling body, or some other skull, would have touched the string so ready to vibrate. But in each case there was a great step of anticipation; Oken thought he saw a type of the whole skeleton in a single vertebra, while Newton conceived at once that the whole universe was full of bodies tending to fall.... The discovery of Goethe, which did for the vegetable kingdom what Oken did for the animal, that the parts of a plant are to be regarded as metamorphosed leaves, is an apparent exception to the necessity of discipline for invention, since it was the discovery of a poet in a region to which he seemed to have paid no especial or laborious attention. But Goethe was himself most anxious to rest the basis of this discovery upon his observation rather than his imagination, and doubtless with good reason.... As with other great discoveries, hints had been given already, though not pursued, both of Goethe's and Oken's principles. Goethe left his to be followed up by others, and but for his great fame, perhaps his name would never have been connected with it. Oken had amassed all the materials necessary for the establishment of his theory; he was able at once to discover and conquer the new territory."

It must not be supposed, however, that all hypotheses flashing into the field of consciousness from the Subconsciousness, are necessarily true or correct. On the contrary many of them are incorrect, or at least only partially correct. The Subconsciousness is not infallible or omniscient—it merely produces results according to the material furnished it. But even these faulty hypotheses are often of value in the later formation of a correct one. As Whewell says: "To try wrong guesses is with most persons the only way to hit upon right ones." Kepler is said to have erected at least twenty hypotheses regarding the shape of the earth's orbit before he finally evolved the correct one. As Brooks says: "Even incorrect hypotheses may be of use in scientific research, since they may lead to more correct suppositions." The supposition of the circular motions of the heavenly bodies around the earth as a center, which lead to the conception of epicycles, etc., and at last to the true theory is an illustration of this. So the 'theory of phlogiston' in chemistry, made many facts intelligible, before the true one of 'oxidation' superseded it. And so, as Thomson says, "with the theory that 'Nature abhors a vacuum,' which served to bring together so many cognate facts not previously considered as related. Even an incorrect conception of this kind has its place in science, so long as it is applicable to the facts; when facts occur which it cannot explain, we either correct it or replace it with a new one. The pathway of science, some one remarks, is strewn with the remains of discarded hypotheses."

Halleck says regarding the danger of hasty inference: "Men must constantly employ imperfect induction in order to advance; but great dangers attend inductive inferences made from too narrow experience. A child has experience with one or two dogs at his home. Because of their gentleness, he argues that all dogs are gentle. He does not, perhaps, find out the contrary until he has been severely bitten. His induction was too hasty. He had not tested a sufficiently large number of dogs to form such a conclusion. From one or two experiences with a large crop in a certain latitude, a farmer may argue that the crop will generally be profitable, whereas it may not again prove so for years. A man may have trusted a number of people and found them honest. He concludes that people as a rule are honest, trusts a certain dishonest man, and is ruined. The older people grow, the more cautious they generally become in forming inductive conclusions. Many instances are noted and compared; but even the wisest sometimes make mistakes. It once was a generally accepted fact that all swans were white. Nobody had ever seen a dark swan, and the inference that all swans were white was regarded as certainly true. Black swans were, however, found in Australia."

Brooks says regarding the probability of hypotheses: "The probability of a hypothesis is in proportion to the number of facts and phenomena it will explain. The larger the number of facts and phenomena that it will satisfactorily account for, the greater our faith in the correctness of our supposition.... If there is more than one hypothesis in respect to the facts under consideration, that one which accounts for the greatest number of facts is the most probable.... In order to verify a hypothesis it must be shown that it will account for all the facts and phenomena. If these facts are numerous and varied, and the subject is so thoroughly investigated that it is quite certain that no important class of facts has been overlooked, the supposition is regarded as true, and the hypothesis is said to be verified. Thus the hypothesis of the 'daily rotation' of the earth on its axis to account for the succession of day and night is accepted as absolutely true. This is the view taken by Dr. Whewell and many other thinkers in respect to the verification of a hypothesis. Some writers, however, as Mill and his school, maintain that in order to verify a hypothesis, we must show not only that it explains all the facts and phenomena, but that there is no other possible hypothesis which will account for them.... The former view of verification is regarded as the correct one. By the latter view, it is evident that a hypothesis could never be verified."

Jevons says: "In the fourth step (verification), we proceed to compare these deductions with the facts already collected, or when necessary and practicable, we make new observations and plan new experiments, so as to find out whether the hypothesis agrees with nature. If we meet with several distinct disagreements between our deductions and our observations, it will become likely that the hypothesis is wrong, and we must then invent a new one. In order to produce agreement it will sometimes be enough to change the hypothesis in a small degree. When we get hold of a hypothesis which seems to give results agreeing with a few facts, we must not at once assume that it is certainly correct. We must go on making other deductions from it under various circumstances, and, whenever it is possible, we ought to verify these results, that is, compare them with facts observed through the senses. When a hypothesis is shown in this way to be true in a great many of its results, especially when it enables us to predict what we should never otherwise have believed or discovered, it becomes certain that the hypothesis itself is a true one.... Sometimes it will happen that two or even three quite different hypotheses all seem to agree with certain facts, so that we are puzzled which to select.... When there are thus two hypotheses, one as good as the other, we need to discover some fact or thing which will agree with one hypothesis and not with the other, because this immediately enables us to decide that the former hypothesis is true and the latter false."

In the above statements regarding the verification of hypotheses we see references made to the testing of the latter upon the "facts" of the case. These facts may be either the observed phenomena or facts apparent to the perception, or else facts obtained by deductive reasoning. The latter may be said to be facts which are held to be true if the hypothesis be true. Thus if we erect the hypothesis that "All men are mortal," we may reason deductively that it will follow that each and every thing that is a man must die sooner or later. Then we test our hypotheses upon each and every man whom we may subject to observation and experiment. If we find a single man who does not die, then the test disproves our hypotheses; if on the contrary all men (the "facts" in the case) prove to be mortal, then is our hypotheses proven or established. The deductive reasoning in this case is as follows: "If so-and-so is true regarding such-and-such a class; and if this particular thing belongs to that class; then it will follow that so-and-so is true regarding this particular thing." This argument is expressed in what is called a Hypothetical Proposition (see Chapter IX), the consideration of which forms a part of the general subject of Deductive Reasoning. Therefore as Jevons has said, "Deductive Reasoning is the Third Step in Inductive Reasoning, and precedes Verification", which we have already considered. Halleck says: "After Induction has classified certain phenomena and thus given us a major premise, we may proceed deductively to apply the inference to any new specimen that can be shown to belong to that class. Induction hands over to deduction a ready-made major premise.... Deduction takes that as a fact, making no inquiry about its truth.... Only after general laws have been laid down, after objects have been classified, after major premises have been formed, can deduction be employed."

In view of the above facts, we shall now proceed to a consideration of that great class of Reasoning known under the term— Deductive Reasoning.

CHAPTER XV.
DEDUCTIVE REASONING

We have seen that there are two great classes of reasoning, known respectively, as (1) Inductive Reasoning, or the discovery of general truth from particular truths; and (2) Deductive Reasoning, or the discovery of particular truths from general truths.

As we have said, Deductive Reasoning is the process of discovering particular truths from a general truth. Thus from the general truth embodied in the proposition "All horses are animals," when it is considered in connection with the secondary proposition that "Dobbin is a horse," we are able to deduce the particular truth that: "Dobbin is an animal." Or, in the following case we deduce a particular truth from a general truth, as follows: "All mushrooms are good to eat; this fungus is a mushroom; therefore, this fungus is good to eat." A deductive argument is expressed in a deductive syllogism.

Jevons says regarding the last stated illustration: "Here are three sentences which state three different facts; but when we know the two first facts, we learn or gather the third fact from the other two. When we thus learn one fact from other facts, we infer or reason, and we do this in the mind. Reasoning thus enables us to ascertain the nature of a thing without actual trial. If we always needed to taste a thing before we could know whether it was good to eat or not, cases of poisoning would be alarmingly frequent. But the appearance and peculiarities of a mushroom may be safely learned by the eye or the nose, and reasoning upon this information and the fact already well known, that mushrooms are good to eat, we arrive without any danger or trouble at the conclusion that the particular fungus before us is good to eat. To reason, then, is to get some knowledge from other knowledge."

The student will recognize that Deductive Reasoning is essentially an analytic process, because it operates in the direction of analyzing a universal or general truth into its particulars—into the particular parts which are included within it—and asserting of them that "what is true of the general is true of the particular." Thus in the general truth that "All men are mortal," we see included the particular truth that "John Smith is mortal"—John Smith having been discovered to be a man. We deduce the particular truth about John Smith from the general truth about "all men." We analyze "all men" and find John Smith to be one of its particular parts. Therefore, "Deduction is an inference from the whole to its parts; that is, an analytic process."

The student will also recognize that Deductive Reasoning is essentially a descending process, because it operates in the direction of a descent from the universal to the particular; from the higher to the lower; from the broader to the narrower. As Brooks says: "Deduction descends from higher truths to lower truths, from laws to facts, from causes to phenomena, etc. Given the law, we can by deduction descend to the facts that fall under the law, even if we have never before seen the facts; and so from the cause we may pass down to observed and even unknown phenomena."

The general truths which are used as the basis of Deductive Reasoning are discovered in several ways. The majority arise from Inductive Reasoning, based upon experience, observation and experiment. For instance in the examples given above, we could not truthfully assert our belief that: "All horses are animals" unless we had previously studied both the horse and animals in general. Nor without this study could we state that "Dobbin is a horse." Nor could we, without previous study, experience and experiment truthfully assert that: "All mushrooms are good to eat;" or that "this fungus is a mushroom;" and that "therefore, this fungus is good to eat." Even as it is, we must be sure that the fungus really is a mushroom, else we run a risk of poisoning ourselves. General truths of this kind are not intuitive, by any means, but are based upon our own experience or the experience of others.

There is a class of general truths which are called intuitive by some authorities. Halleck says of these: "Some psychologists claim that we have knowledge obtained neither through induction nor deduction; that we recognize certain truths the moment we perceive certain objects, without any process of inference. Under the head of intuitive knowledge are classified such cases as the following: We perceive an object and immediately know that it is a time relation, as existing now and then. We are said to have an intuitive concept of time. When we are told that the whole is greater than a part; that things equal to the same thing are equal to each other; that a straight line cannot enclose space, we immediately, or intuitively, recognize the truth of these statements. Attempts at proof do not make us feel surer of their truth.... We say that it is self-evident, or that we know the fact intuitively. The axioms of mathematics and logic are said to be intuitive."

Another class of authorities, however, deny the nature of intuitive knowledge of truth, or intuitive truths. They claim that all our ideas arise from sensation and reflection, and that what we call "intuition" is merely the result of sensation and reflection reproduced by memory or heredity. They hold that the intuitions of animals and men are simply the representation of experiences of the race, or individual, arising from the impressions stored away in the subconsciousness of the individual. Halleck states regarding this: "This school likens intuition to instinct. It grants that the young duck knows water instinctively, plunges into it, and swims without learning. These psychologists believe that there was a time when this was not the case with the progenitors of the duck. They had to gain this knowledge slowly through experience. Those that learned the proper aquatic lesson survived and transmitted this knowledge through a modified structure, to their progeny. Those that failed in the lesson perished in the struggle for existence.... This school claims that the intuition of cause and effect arose in the same way. Generations of human beings have seen the cause invariably joined to the effect; hence, through inseparable association came the recognition of their necessary sequence. The tendency to regard all phenomena in these relations was with steadily increasing force transmitted by the laws of heredity to posterity, until the recognition of the relationship has become an intuition."

Another class of general truths is merely hypothetical. Hypothetical means "Founded on or including a hypothesis or supposition; assumed or taken for granted, though not proved, for the purpose of deducing proofs of a point in question." The hypotheses and theories of physical science are used as general truths for deductive reasoning. Hypothetical general truths are in the nature of premises assumed in order to proceed with the process of Deductive Reasoning, and without which such reasoning would be impossible. They are, however, as a rule not mere assumptions, but are rather in the nature of assumptions rendered plausible by experience, experiment and Inductive Reasoning. The Law of Gravitation may be considered hypothetical, and yet it is the result of Inductive Reasoning based upon a vast multitude of facts and phenomena.

The Primary Basis of Deductive Reasoning may be said to rest upon the logical axiom, which has come down to us from the ancients, and which is stated as follows: "Whatever is true of the whole is true of its parts." Or, as later authorities have expressed it: "Whatever is true of the general is true of the particular." This axiom is the basis upon which we build our Deductive Reasoning. It furnishes us with the validity of the deductive inference or argument. If we are challenged for proof of the statement that "This fungus is good to eat," we are able to answer that we are justified in making the statement by the self-evident proposition, or axiom, that "Whatever is true of the general is true of the particular." If the general "mushroom" is good to eat, then the particular, "this fungus" being a mushroom, must also be good to eat. All horses (general) being animals, then according to the axiom, Dobbin (particular horse) must also be an animal.

This axiom has been stated in various terms other than those stated above. For instance: "Whatever may be affirmed or denied of the whole, may be denied or affirmed of the parts;" which form is evidently derived from that used by Hamilton who said: "What belongs, or does not belong, to the containing whole, belongs or does not belong, to each of the contained parts." Aristotle formulated his celebrated Dictum as follows: "Whatever can be predicated affirmatively or negatively of any class or term distributed, can be predicated in like manner of all and singular the classes or individuals contained under it."

There is another form of Deductive Reasoning, that is a form based upon another axiom than that of: "Whatever is true of the whole is true of the parts." This form of reasoning is sometimes called Mathematical Reasoning, because it is the form of reasoning employed in mathematics. Its axiom is stated as follows: "Things which are equal to the same thing, are equal to one another." It will be seen that this is the principle employed in mathematics. Thus: "x equals y; and y equals 5; therefore, x equals 5." Or stated in logical terms: "A equals B; B equals C; therefore, A equals C." Thus it is seen that this form of reasoning, as well as the ordinary form of Deductive Reasoning, is strictly mediate, that is, made through the medium of a third thing, or "two things being compared through their relation to a third."

Brooks states: "The real reason for the certainty of mathematical reasoning may be stated as follows: First, its ideas are definite, necessary, and exact conceptions of quantity. Second, its definitions, as the description of these ideas are necessary, exact, and indisputable truths. Third, the axioms from which we derive conclusions by comparison are all self-evident and necessary truths. Comparing these exact ideas by the necessary laws of inference, the result must be absolutely true. Or, stated in another way, using these definitions and axioms as the premises of a syllogism, the conclusion follows inevitably. There is no place or opportunity for error to creep in to mar or vitiate our derived truths."

In conclusion, we wish to call your attention to a passage from Jevons which is worthy of consideration and recollection. Jevons says: "There is a simple rule which will enable us to test the truth of a great many arguments, even of many which do not come under any of the rules commonly given in books on logic. This rule is that whatever is true of one term is true of any term which is stated to be the same in meaning as that term. In other words, we may always substitute one term for another if we know that they refer to exactly the same thing. There is no doubt that a horse is some animal, and therefore the head of a horse is the head of some animal. This argument cannot be brought under the rules of the syllogism, because it contains four distinct logical terms in two propositions; namely, horse, some animal; head of horse, head of some animal. But it easily comes under the rule which I have given, because we have simply to put 'some animal' instead of 'a horse'. A great many arguments may be explained in this way. Gold is a metal; therefore a piece of gold is a piece of metal. A negro is a fellow creature; therefore, he who strikes a negro, strikes a fellow creature."

The same eminent authority says: "When we examine carefully enough the way in which we reason, it will be found in every case to consist in putting one thing or term in place of another, to which we know it to have an exact resemblance in some respect. We use the likeness as a kind of bridge, which leads us from a knowledge of one thing to a knowledge of another; thus the true principle of reasoning may be called the substitution of similars, or the passing from like to like. We infer the character of one thing from the character of something which acts as a go-between, or third term. When we are certain there is an exact likeness, our inference is certain; when we only believe that there probably is, or guess that there is, then our inferences are only probable, not certain."

CHAPTER XVI.
THE SYLLOGISM

The third and highest phase or step in reasoning—the step which follows after those styled Conception and Judgment—is generally known by the general term "Reasoning," which term, however, is used to include the two precedent steps as well as the final step itself. This step or process consists of the comparing of two objects, persons or things, through their relation to a third object, person or thing. As, for instance, we reason (a) that all mammals are animals; (b) that a horse is a mammal; and (c) that, therefore, a horse is an animal. The most fundamental principle of this step or reasoning consists in the comparing of two objects of thought through and by means of their relation to a third object. The natural form of expression of this process of reasoning is called a "Syllogism."

The process of reasoning which gives rise to the expression of the argument in the form of a Syllogism must be understood if one wishes to form a clear conception of the Syllogism. The process itself is very simple when plainly stated, although the beginner is sometimes puzzled by the complicated definitions and statements of the authorities. Let us suppose that we have three objects, A, B and C, respectively. We wish to compare C and B, but fail to establish a relation between them at first. We however are able to establish a relation between A and B; and between C and A. We thus have the two propositions (1) "A equals B; and (2) C equals A". The next step is that of inferring that "if A equals B, and C equals A, then it must follow, logically, that C equals B." This process is that of indirect or mediate comparison, rather than immediate. C and B are not compared directly or immediately, but indirectly and through the medium of A. A is thus said to mediate between B and C.

This process of reasoning embraces three ideas or objects of thought, in their expression of propositions. It comprises the fundamental or elemental form of reasoning. As Brooks says: "The simplest movement of the reasoning process is the comparing of two objects through their relation to a third." The result of this process is an argument expressed in what is called a Syllogism. Whately says that: "A Syllogism is an argument expressed in strict logical form so that its conclusiveness is manifest from the structure of the expression alone, without any regard to the meaning of the terms." Brooks says: "All reasoning can be and naturally is expressed in the form of the syllogism. It applies to both inductive and deductive reasoning, and is the form in which these processes are presented. Its importance as an instrument of thought requires that it receive special notice."

In order that the nature and use of the Syllogism may be clearly understood, we can do no better than to at once present for your consideration the well-known "Rules of the Syllogism," an understanding of which carries with it a perfect comprehension of the Syllogism itself.

The Rules of the Syllogism state that in order for a Syllogism to be a perfect Syllogism, it is necessary:

I. That there should be three, and no more than three, Propositions. These three propositions are: (1) the Conclusion, or thing to be proved; and (2 and 3) the Premises, or the means of proving the Conclusion, and which are called the Major Premise and Minor Premise, respectively. We may understand this more clearly if we will examine the following example:

Major Premise: "Man is mortal;" (or "A is B").

Minor Premise: "Socrates is a man;" (or "C is A"). Therefore:

Conclusion: "Socrates is mortal" (or "C is B").

It will be seen that the above Syllogism, whether expressed in words or symbols, is logically valid, because the conclusion must logically follow the premises. And, in this case, the premises being true, it must follow that the conclusion is true. Whately says: "A Syllogism is said to be valid when the conclusion logically follows from the premises; if the conclusion does not so follow, the Syllogism is invalid and constitutes a Fallacy, if the error deceives the reasoner himself; but if it is advanced with the idea of deceiving others it constitutes a Sophism."

The reason for Rule I is that only three propositions—a Major Premise, a Minor Premise, and a Conclusion—are needed to form a Syllogism. If we have more than three propositions, then we must have more than two premises from which to draw one conclusion. The presence of more than two premises would result in the formation of two or more Syllogisms, or else in the failure to form a Syllogism.

II. That there should be three and no more than three Terms. These Terms are (1) The Predicate of the Conclusion; (2) the Subject of the Conclusion; and (3) the Middle Term which must occur in both premises, being the connecting link in bringing the two other Terms together in the Conclusion.

The Predicate of the Conclusion is called the Major Term, because it is the greatest in extension compared with its fellow terms. The Subject of the Conclusion is called the Minor Term because it is the smallest in extension compared with its fellow terms. The Major and Minor Terms are called the Extremes. The Middle Term operates between the two Extremes.

The Major Term and the Middle Term must appear in the Major

Premise.

The Minor Term and the Middle Term must appear in the Minor Premise.

The Minor Term and the Major Term must appear in the Conclusion.

Thus we see that The Major Term must be the Predicate of the Conclusion; the Minor Term the Subject of the Conclusion; the Middle Term may be the Subject or Predicate of either of the premises, but must always be found once in both premises.

The following example will show this arrangement more clearly:

In the Syllogism: "Man is mortal; Socrates is a man; therefore Socrates is mortal," we have the following arrangement: "Mortal," the Major Term; "Socrates," the Minor Term; and "Man," the Middle Term; as follows:

Major Premise: "Man" (middle term) is mortal (major term).

Minor Premise: "Socrates" (minor term) is a man (major term).

Conclusion: "Socrates" (minor term) is mortal (major term).

The reason for the rule that there shall be "only three" terms is that reasoning consists in comparing two terms with each other through the medium of a third term. There must be three terms; if there are more than three terms, we form two syllogisms instead of one.

III. That one premise, at least, must be affirmative. This, because "from two negative propositions nothing can be inferred." A negative proposition asserts that two things differ, and if we have two propositions so asserting difference, we can infer nothing from them. If our Syllogism stated that: (1) "Man is not mortal;" and (2) that "Socrates is not a man;" we could form no Conclusion, either that Socrates was or was not mortal. There would be no logical connection between the two premises, and therefore no Conclusion could be deduced therefrom. Therefore, at least one premise must be affirmative.

IV. If one premise is negative, the conclusion must be negative. This because "if one term agrees and another disagrees with a third term, they must disagree with each other." Thus if our Syllogism stated that: (1) "Man is not mortal;" and (2) that: "Socrates is a man;" we must announce the Negative Conclusion that: (3) "Socrates is not mortal."

V. That the Middle Term must be distributed; (that is, taken universally) in at least one premise. This "because, otherwise, the Major Term may be compared with one part of the Middle Term, and the Minor Term with another part of the latter; and there will be actually no common Middle Term, and consequently no common ground for an inference." The violation of this rule causes what is commonly known as "The Undistributed Middle," a celebrated Fallacy condemned by the logicians. In the Syllogism mentioned as an example in this chapter, the proposition "Man is mortal," really means "All men," that is, Man in his universal sense. Literally the proposition is "All men are mortal," from which it is seen that Socrates being "a man" (or some of all men) must partake of the quality of the universal Man. If the Syllogism, instead, read: "Some men are mortal," it would not follow that Socrates must be mortal—he might or might not be so. Another form of this fallacy is shown in the statement that (1) White is a color; (2) Black is a color; hence (3) Black must be White. The two premises really mean "White is some color;

Black is some color;" and not that either is "all colors." Another example is: "Men are bipeds; birds are bipeds; hence, men are birds." In this example "bipeds" is not distributed as "all bipeds" but is simply not-distributed as "some bipeds." These syllogisms, therefore, not being according to rule, must fail. They are not true syllogisms, and constitute fallacies.

To be "distributed," the Middle Term must be the Subject of a Universal Proposition, or the Predicate of a Negative Proposition; to be "undistributed" it must be the Subject of a Particular Proposition, or the Predicate of an Affirmative Proposition. (See chapter on Propositions.)

VI. That an extreme, if undistributed in a Premise, may not be distributed in the Conclusion. This because it would be illogical and unreasonable to assert more in the conclusion than we find in the premises. It would be most illogical to argue that: (1) "All horses are animals; (2) no man is a horse; therefore (3) no man is an animal." The conclusion would be invalid, because the term animal is distributed in the conclusion, (being the predicate of a negative proposition) while it is not distributed in the premise (being the predicate of an affirmative proposition).

As we have said before, any Syllogism which violates any of the above six syllogisms is invalid and a fallacy.

There are two additional rules which may be called derivative. Any syllogism which violates either of these two derivative rules, also violates one or more of the first six rules as given above in detail.

The Two Derivative Rules of the Syllogism are as follows:

VII. That one Premise at least must be Universal. This because "from two particular premises no conclusion can be drawn."

VIII. That if one premise is Particular, the Conclusion must be particular also. This because only a universal conclusion can be drawn from two universal premises.

The principles involved in these two Derivative Rules may be tested by stating Syllogisms violating them. They contain the essence of the other rules, and every syllogism which breaks them will be found to also break one or more of the other rules given.

CHAPTER XVII.
VARIETIES OF SYLLOGISMS

The authorities in Logic hold that with the four kinds of propositions grouped in every possible order of arrangement, it is possible to form nineteen different kinds of valid arguments, which are called the nineteen moods of the syllogism. These are classified by division into what are called the four figures, each of which figures may be known by the position of the middle term in the premises. Logicians have arranged elaborate and curious tables constructed to show what kinds of propositions when joined in a particular order of arrangement will make sound and valid syllogisms. We shall not set forth these tables here, as they are too technical for a popular presentation of the subject before us, and because they are not necessary to the student who will thoroughly familiarize himself with the above stated Laws of the Syllogism and who will therefore be able to determine in every case whether any given argument is a correct syllogism, or otherwise.

In many instances of ordinary thought and expression the complete syllogistic form is omitted, or not stated at full length. It is common usage to omit one premise of a syllogism, in ordinary expression, the missing premise being inferred by the speaker and hearer. A syllogism with one premise unexpressed is sometimes called an Enthymene, the term meaning "in the mind." For instance, the following: "We are a free people, therefore we are happy," the major premise "All free people are happy" being omitted or unexpressed. Also in "Poets are imaginative, therefore Byron was imaginative," the minor premise "Byron was a poet" is omitted or unexpressed. Jevons says regarding this phase of the subject: "Thus in the Sermon on the Mount, the verses known as the Beatitudes consist each of one premise and a conclusion, and the conclusion is put first. 'Blessed are the merciful: for they shall obtain mercy.' The subject and the predicate of the conclusion are here inverted, so that the proposition is really 'The merciful are blessed.' It is evidently understood that 'All who shall obtain mercy are blessed,' so that the syllogism, when stated at full length, becomes: 'All who shall obtain mercy are blessed; All who are merciful shall obtain mercy; Therefore, all who are merciful are blessed.' This is a perfectly good syllogism."

Whenever we find any of the words: "because, for, therefore, since," or similar terms, we may know that there is an argument, and usually a syllogism.

We have seen that there are three special kinds of Propositions, namely, (1) Categorical Propositions, or propositions in which the affirmation or denial is made without reservation or qualification; (2) Hypothetical Propositions, in which the affirmation or denial is made to depend upon certain conditions, circumstances, or suppositions; and (3) Disjunctive Propositions, in which is implied or asserted an alternative.

The forms of reasoning based upon these three several classes of propositions bear the same names as the latter. And, accordingly the respective syllogisms expressing these forms of reasoning also bear the class name or term. Thus, a Categorical Syllogism is one containing only categorical propositions; a Hypothetical Syllogism is one containing one or more hypothetical propositions; a Disjunctive Syllogism is one containing a disjunctive proposition in the major premise.

Categorical Syllogisms, which are far more common than the other two kinds, have been considered in the previous chapter, and the majority of the examples of syllogisms given in this book are of this kind. In a Categorical Syllogism the statement or denial is made positively, and without reservation or qualification, and the reasoning thereupon partakes of the same positive character. In propositions or syllogisms of this kind it is asserted or assumed that the premise is true and correct, and, if the reasoning be logically correct it must follow that the conclusion is correct, and the new proposition springing therefrom must likewise be Categorical in its nature.

Hypothetical Syllogisms, on the contrary, have as one or more of their premises a hypothetical proposition which affirms or asserts something provided, or "if," something else be true. Hyslop says of this: "Often we wish first to bring out, if only conditionally, the truth upon which a proposition rests, so as to see if the connection between this conclusion and the major premise be admitted. The whole question will then depend upon the matter of treating the minor premise. This has the advantage of getting the major premise admitted without the formal procedure of proof, and the minor premise is usually more easily proved than the major. Consequently, one is made to see more clearly the force of the argument or reasoning by removing the question of the material truth of the major premise and concentrating attention upon the relation between the conclusion and its conditions, so that we know clearly what we have first to deny if we do not wish to accept it."

By joining a hypothetical proposition with an ordinary proposition we create a Hypothetical Proposition. For instance: "If York contains a cathedral it is a city; York does contain a cathedral; therefore, York is a city." Or: "If dogs have four feet, they are quadrupeds; dogs do have four feet; therefore dogs are quadrupeds." The Hypothetical Syllogism may be either affirmative or negative; that is, its hypothetical proposition may either hypothetically affirm or hypothetically deny. The part of the premise of a Hypothetical Syllogism which conditions or questions (and which usually contains the little word "if") is called the Antecedent. The major premise is the one usually thus conditioned. The other part of the conditioned proposition, and which part states what will happen or is true under the conditional circumstances, is called the Consequent. Thus, in one of the above examples: "If dogs have four feet" is the Antecedent; and the remainder of the proposition: "they are quadrupeds" is the Consequent. The Antecedent is indicated by the presence of some conditional term as: if, supposing, granted that, provided that, although, had, were, etc., the general sense and meaning of such terms being that of the little word "if." The Consequent has no special indicating term.

Jevons gives the following clear and simple Rules regarding the Hypothetical Syllogism:

I. "If the Antecedent be affirmed, the consequent may be affirmed. If the Consequent be denied, the Antecedent may be denied."

II. "Avoid the fallacy of affirming the consequent, or denying the antecedent. This is a fallacy because of the fact that the conditional statement made in the major premise may not be the only one determining the consequent." The following is an example of "Affirming the Consequent:" "If it is raining, the sky is overclouded; the sky is overclouded; therefore, it is raining." In truth, the sky may be overclouded, and still it may not be raining. The fallacy is still more apparent when expressed in symbols, as follows: "If A is B, C is D; C is D; therefore, A is B." The fallacy of denying the Antecedent is shown by the following example: "If Radium were cheap it would be useful; Radium is not cheap; therefore Radium is not useful." Or, expressed in symbols: "If A is B, C is D; A is not B; therefore C is not D." In truth Radium may be useful although not cheap. Jevons gives the following examples of these fallacies: "If a man is a good teacher, he thoroughly understands his subject; but John Jones thoroughly understands his subject; therefore, he is a good teacher." Also, "If snow is mixed with salt it melts; the snow on the ground is not mixed with salt; therefore it does not melt."

Jevons says: "To affirm the consequent and then to infer that we can affirm the antecedent, is as bad as breaking the third rule of the syllogism, and allowing an undistributed middle term.... To deny the antecedent is really to break the fourth rule of the syllogism, and to take a term as distributed in the conclusion which was not so in the premises."

Hypothetical Syllogisms may usually be easily reduced to or converted into Categorical Syllogisms. As Jevons says: "In reality, hypothetical propositions and syllogisms are not different from those which we have more fully considered. It is all a matter of the convenience of stating the propositions." For instance, instead of saying: "If Radium were cheap, it would be useful," we may say "Cheap Radium would be useful;" or instead of saying: "If glass is thin, it breaks easily," we may say "Thin glass breaks easily." Hyslop gives the following Rule for Conversion in such cases: "Regard the antecedent of the hypothetical proposition as the subject of the categorical, and the consequent of the hypothetical proposition as the predicate of the categorical. In some cases this change is a very simple one; in others it can be effected only by a circumlocution."

The third class of syllogisms, known as The Disjunctive Syllogism, is the exception to the law which holds that all good syllogisms must fit in and come under the Rules of the Syllogism, as stated in the preceding chapter. Not only does it refuse to obey these Rules, but it fails to resemble the ordinary syllogism in many ways. As Jevons says: "It would be a great mistake to suppose that all good logical arguments must obey the rules of the syllogism, which we have been considering. Only those arguments which connect two terms together by means of a middle term, and are therefore syllogisms, need obey these rules. A great many of the arguments which we daily use are of this nature; but there are a great many other kinds of arguments, some of which have never been understood by logicians until recent years. One important kind of argument is known as the Disjunctive Syllogism, though it does not obey the rules of the syllogism, or in any way resemble syllogisms."

The Disjunctive Syllogism is one having a disjunctive proposition in its major premise. The disjunctive proposition also appears in the conclusion when the disjunction in the major premise happens to contain more than two terms. A disjunctive proposition, we have seen, is one which possesses alternative predicates for the subject in which the conjunction "or" (sometimes accompanied by "either") appears. As for instance: "Lightning is sheet or forked;" or, "Arches are either round or pointed;" or, "Angles are either obtuse, or right angled, or acute." The different things joined together by "or" are called Alternatives, the term indicating that we may choose between the things, and that if one will not answer our purpose we may take the other, or one of the others if there be more than one other.

The Rule regarding the Use of Disjunctive Syllogisms is that: "If one or more alternatives be denied, the rest may still be affirmed." Thus if we say that "A is B or C," or that "A is either B or C," we may deny the B but still affirm the C. Some authorities also hold that "If we affirm one alternative, we must deny the remainder," but this view is vigorously disputed by other authorities. It would seem to be a valid rule in cases where the term "either" appears as: "A is either B or C," because there seems to be an implication that one or the other alone can be true. But in cases like: "A is B or C," there may be a possibility of both being true. Jevons takes this latter view, giving as an example the proposition: "A Magistrate is a Justice-of-the-Peace, a Mayor, or

104

a Stipendiary Magistrate," but it does not follow that one who is a Justice-of-the-Peace may not be at the same time a Mayor. He states: "After affirming one alternative we can only deny the others if there be such a difference between them that they could not be true at the same time." It would seem that both contentions are at the same time true, the example given by Jevons illustrating his contention, and the proposition "The prisoner is either guilty or innocent" illustrating the contentions of the other side.

A Dilemma is a conditional syllogism whose Major Premise presents some sort of alternative. Whately defines it as: "A conditional syllogism with two or more antecedents in the major, and a disjunctive minor." There being two mutually exclusive propositions in the Major Premise, the reasoner is compelled to admit one or the other, and is then caught between "the two horns of the dilemma."

CHAPTER XVIII.
REASONING BY ANALOGY

What is called Reasoning by Analogy is one of the most elementary forms of reasoning, and the one which the majority of us most frequently employ. It is a primitive form of hasty generalization evidencing in the natural expectation that "things will happen as they have happened before in like circumstances." The term as used in logic has been defined as "Resemblance of relations; Resemblances of any kind on which an argument falling short of induction may be founded." Brooks says: "Analogy is that process of thought by which we infer that if two things resemble each other in one or more particulars, they will resemble each other in some other particular."

Jevons states the Rule for Reasoning by Analogy, as follows: "If two or more things resemble each other in many points, they will probably resemble each other also in more points." Others have stated the same principle as follows: "When one thing resembles another in known particulars, it will resemble it also in the unknown;" and "If two things agree in several particulars, they will also agree in other particulars."

There is a difference between generalization by induction, and by analogy. In inductive generalization the rule is: "What is true of the many is true of all;" while the rule of analogy is: "things that have some things in common have other things in common." As Jevons aptly remarks: "Reasoning by Analogy differs only in degree from that kind of reasoning called 'Generalization.' When many things resemble each other in a few properties, we argue about them by Generalization. When a few things resemble each other in many properties, it is a case of analogy." Illustrating Analogy, we may say that if in A we find the qualities, attributes or properties called a, b, c, d, e, f, g, respectively, and if we find that in B the qualities, etc., called a, b, c, d, e, respectively, are present, then we may reason by analogy that the qualities f and g must also belong to B.

Brooks says of this form of reasoning: "This principle is in constant application in ordinary life and in science. A physician, in visiting a patient, says this disease corresponds in several particulars with typhoid fever, hence it will correspond in all particulars, and is typhoid fever. So, when the geologist discovers a fossil animal with large, strong, blunt claws, he infers that it procured its food by scratching or burrowing in the earth. It was by analogy that Dr. Buckland constructed an animal from a few fossil bones, and when subsequently the bones of the entire animal were discovered, his construction was found to be correct." Halleck says: "In argument or reasoning we are much aided by the habit of searching for hidden resemblances.... The detection of such a relation cultivates thought. If we are to succeed in argument, we must develop what some call a sixth sense of such relations.... The study of poetry may be made very serviceable in detecting analogies and cultivating the reasoning powers. When the poet brings clearly to mind the change due to death, using as an illustration the caterpillar body transformed into the butterfly spirit, moving with winged ease over flowering meadows, he is cultivating our apprehension of relations, none the less valuable because they are beautiful."

But the student must be on guard against the deceptive conclusions sometimes arising from Reasoning by Analogy. As Jevons says: "In many cases Reasoning by Analogy is found to be a very uncertain guide. In some cases unfortunate mistakes are made. Children are sometimes killed by gathering and eating poisonous berries, wrongly inferring that they can be eaten, because other berries, of a somewhat similar appearance, have been found agreeable and harmless. Poisonous toadstools are occasionally mistaken for mushrooms, especially by people not accustomed to gathering them. In Norway mushrooms are seldom seen, and are not eaten; but when I once found a few there and had them cooked at an inn, I was amused by the people of the inn, who went and collected toadstools and wanted me to eat them also. This was clearly a case of mistaken reasoning by analogy. Even brute animals reason in the same way in some degree. The beaten dog fears every stick, and there are few dogs which will not run away when you pretend to pick up a stone, even if there be no stone to pick up." Halleck says: "Many false analogies are manufactured, and it is excellent thought training to expose them. The majority of people think so little that they swallow these false analogies just as newly fledged robins swallow small stones dropped into their open mouths.... This tendency to think as others do must be resisted somewhere along the line, or there can be no progress." Brooks says: "The argument from Analogy is plausible, but often deceptive. Thus to infer that since American swans are white, the Australian swan is white, gives a false conclusion, for it is really black. So to infer that because John Smith has a red nose and is a drunkard, then Henry Jones who also has a red nose is also a drunkard, would be a dangerous inference.... Conclusions of this kind drawn from analogy are frequently fallacious."

Regarding the Rule for Reasoning from Analogy, Jevons says: "There is no way in which we can really assure ourselves that we are arguing safely by analogy. The only rule that can be given is this; that the more closely two things resemble each other, the more likely it is that they are the same in other respects, especially in points closely connected with those observed.... In order to be clear about our conclusions, we ought in fact never to rest satisfied with mere analogy, but ought to try to discover the general laws governing the case. In analogy we seem to reason from one fact to another fact without troubling ourselves either with deduction or induction. But it is only by a kind of guess that we do so; it is not really conclusive reasoning. We ought properly to ascertain what general laws of nature are shown to exist by the facts observed, and then infer what will happen according to these laws.... We find that reasoning by analogy is not to be depended upon, unless we make such an inquiry into the causes and laws of the things in question, that we really employ inductive and deductive reasoning."

Along the same lines, Brooks says: "The inference from analogy, like that from induction, should be used with caution. Its conclusion must not be regarded as certain, but merely as reaching a high degree of probability. The inference from a part to a part, no more than from a part to the whole, is attended with any rational necessity. To attain certainty, we must show that the principles which lie at the root of the process are either necessary laws of thought or necessary laws of nature; both of which are impossible. Hence analogy can pretend to only a high degree of probability. It may even reach a large degree of certainty, but it never reaches necessity. We must, therefore, be careful not to accept any inference from analogy as true until it is proved to be true by actual observation and experiment, or by such an application of induction as to remove all reasonable doubt."

CHAPTER XIX.
FALLACIES

A Fallacy is: "An unsound argument or mode of arguing, which, while appearing to be decisive of a question, is in reality not so; an argument or proposition apparently sound, but really fallacious; a fallacious statement or proposition, in which the error is not apparent, and which is therefore likely to mislead or deceive; sophistry."

In Deductive Reasoning, we meet with two classes of Fallacies; namely, (1) Fallacious Premise; and (2) Fallacious Conclusion. We shall now consider each of these in turn.

Fallacious Premise is in effect an unwarranted assumption of premises. One of the most common forms of this kind of Fallacy is known as "Begging the Question," the principle of which is the assumption of a fundamental premise which is not conceded; the unwarrantable assumption of that which is to be proved; or the assumption of that by which it is to be proved, without proving it. Its most common form is that of boldly stating some unproven fact, authoritatively and positively, and then proceeding to use the statement as the major premise of the argument, proceeding logically from that point. The hearer perceiving the argument proceeding logically often fails to remember that the premise has been merely assumed, without warrant and without proof and omitting the hypothetical "if." One may proceed to argue logically from the premise that "The moon is made of green cheese," but the whole argument is invalid and fallacious because of the fact that the person making it has "begged the question" upon an unwarranted premise. Hyslop gives a good example of this form of fallacy in the case of the proposition "Church and State should be united." Proof being demanded the advocate proceeds to "beg the question" as follows: "Good institutions should be united; Church and State are good institutions; therefore, Church and State should be united." The proposition that "Good institutions should be united" is fallacious, being merely assumed and not proven. The proposition sounds reasonable, and few will feel disposed to dispute it at first, but a little consideration will show that while some good institutions may well be united, it is not a general truth that all should be so.

"Begging the Question" also often arises from giving a name to a thing, and then assuming that we have explained the thing. This is a very frequent practice with many people—they try to explain by merely applying names. An example of this kind is had in the case of the person who tried to explain why one could see through a pane of glass by saying "because it is transparent." Or when one explains that the reason a certain substance breaks easily is "because it is brittle." Moliere makes the father of a dumb girl ask why his daughter is dumb. The physician answers: "Nothing is more easy than to explain it; it comes from her having lost the power of speech." "Yes, yes," objects the father, "but the cause, if you please, why she has lost the power of speech." The physician gravely replies: "All our best authors will tell you that it is the impeding of the action of the tongue."

Jevons says: "The most frequent way, perhaps, in which we commit this kind of fallacy is to employ names which imply that we disapprove of something, and then argue that because it is such and such, it must be condemned. When two sportsmen fall out in some manner relating to the subject of game, one will, in all probability, argue that the act of the other was 'unsportsmanlike,' and therefore should not have been done. Here is to all appearance a correct syllogism:

"No unsportsmanlike act should be done; John Robinson's act was unsportsmanlike: Therefore, John Robinson's act should not have been done.

"This is quite correct in form; but it is evidently the mere semblance of an argument. 'Unsportsmanlike' means what a sportsman should not do. The point to be argued was whether the act fell within the customary definition of what was unsportsmanlike."

Arising from "Begging the Question," and in fact a class of the latter, is what is called "Reasoning in a Circle." In this form of fallacy one assumes as proof of a proposition the proposition itself; or, uses the conclusion to prove the premise. For instance: "This man is a rascal because he is a rogue; and he is a rogue because he is a rascal." Or, "It is warm because it is summer; and it is summer because it is warm." Or "He never drinks to excess, because he is never intemperate in drinking."

Brooks says: "Thus to argue that a party is good because it advocates good measures, and that certain measures are good because they are advocated by so excellent a party, is to reason in a circle. So when persons argue that their church is the true one, because it was established by God, and then argue that since it is the true church it must have been founded by God, they fall into this fallacy. To argue that 'the will is determined by the strongest motive' and to define the strongest motive as 'that which influences the will,' is to revolve in a circle of thought and prove nothing. Plato commits this error when he argues the immortality of the soul from its simplicity, and afterwards attempts to prove its simplicity from its immortality." It needs care to avoid this error, for it is surprising how easily one falls into it. Hyslop says: "The fallacy of Reasoning in a Circle occurs mostly in long arguments where it can be committed without ready detection.... When it occurs in a long discourse it may be committed without easy discovery. It is likely to be occasioned by the use of synonyms which are taken to express more than the conception involved when they do not." What is called a Vicious Circle is caused when the conclusion of one syllogism is used for a proposition in another syllogism, which in its turn comes to be used as a basis for the first or original syllogism.

Fallacious Conclusion is in effect an unwarranted or irrelevant assumption of a logical conclusion. There are many forms of this fallacy among which are the following:

Shifting ground, which consists in the pretence of proving one thing while in reality merely a similar or related thing is being proved. In this class is the argument that because a man is profane he must necessarily be dishonest; or that because a man denies the inspiration of the Scriptures he must be an atheist.

Fallacious Questioning, in which two or more related questions are asked, and the answer of one is then applied to the other. For instance: "You assert that the more civilized a community, the more silk-hats are to be found in it?" "Yes." "Then, you state that silk-hats are the promoters and cause of civilization in a community?" A question of this kind is often so arranged that an answer either in the affirmative or the negative will lead to a false or fallacious inference. For instance, the question once asked a respectable citizen on the witness stand: "Have you stopped beating your mother?" An answer of either "Yes" or "No," was out of the question, for it would have placed the witness in a false position, for he had never beaten his mother, nor been accused of the same.

Partial Proof, in which the proof of a partial or related fact is used to infer a proof of the whole fact or a related one. For instance, it is fallacious to argue that a man has been guilty of drunkenness by merely proving that he was seen entering a saloon.

Appeal to Public Opinion, in which the prejudices of the public are appealed to rather than its judgment or reason. In politics and theological argument this fallacy is frequent. It is no argument, and is reprehensible.

Appeal to Authority, or Reverence, in which the reverence and respect of the public for certain persons is used to influence their feelings in place of their judgment or reason. For instance: "Washington thought so-and-so, and therefore it must be right;" or "It is foolish to affirm that Aristotle erred;" or "It has been believed by men for two thousand years, that, etc;" or "What our fathers believed must be true." Appeals of this kind may have their proper place, but they are fallacies nevertheless, and not real argument.

Appeal to Profession, in which an appeal is made to practices, principles or professions of the opponent, rather than to reason or judgment. Thus we may argue that a certain philosophy or religion cannot be sound or good, because certain people who hold it are not consistent, or not worthy, moral or sober. This argument is often used effectively against an opponent, and is valid against him personally. But it is no valid argument against his philosophy or belief, because he may act in violation of them, or he may change his practices and still adhere to his beliefs—the two are not joined.

Appeal to General Belief, in which an appeal is made to general or universal belief, although the same may be unsupported by proof. This is quite common, but is no real argument. The common opinion may be erroneous, as history proves. A few centuries ago this argument could have been used in favor of the earth being flat, etc. A half-century ago it was used against Darwin. Today it is being used against other new ideas. It is a fallacy by its very nature.

Appeal to Ignorance, in which an appeal is made to the ignorance of the opponent that his conviction may follow from his inability to prove the contrary. It is virtually no argument that: "So-and-so must be true, because you cannot prove that it is not." As Brooks says: "To argue that there is no material world, because we cannot explain how the mind knows it to exist, is the celebrated fallacy of Hume in philosophy. The fact that we cannot find a needle in a haystack is no proof that it is not there."

Introduction of New Matter, also called Non Sequitur, in which matter is introduced into the conclusion that is not in the premises. Hyslop gives the following example of it: "All men are rational; Socrates is a man; therefore, Socrates is noble." De Morgan gives the following more complex example: "Episcopacy is of Scripture origin; The Church of England is the only Episcopal church in England; therefore, the church established is the church that ought to be supported."

Other fallacies, resembling in some respects those above mentioned, are as follows:

Fallacy of Ambiguous Terms, in which different meanings of the same word are used to produce the fallacious argument. As Jevons says: "A word with two distinct meanings is really two words."

Confusion between Collective and General Meanings of a Term, of which Jevons says: "It would be obviously absurd to argue that because all the books in the British Museum Library are sure to give information about King Alfred, therefore any particular book will be sure to give it. By 'all the books in the British Museum Library,' we mean all taken together. There are many other cases where the confusion is not so evident, and where great numbers of people are unable to see the exact difference."

Arguing from the Collective to the General, in which the fallacy consists of arguing that because something is true of the whole of a group of things, therefore it is true of any of those things. Jevons says: "All the soldiers in a regiment may be able to capture a town, but it is absurd to suppose that therefore every soldier in the regiment could capture the town single handed. White sheep eat a great deal more than black sheep; but that is because there are so many more of them."

Uncertain Meaning of a Sentence, from which confusion arises and fallacious argument may spring. Jevons says: "There is a humorous way of proving that a cat must have three tails: Because a cat has one tail more than no cat; and no cat has two tails; therefore, any cat has three tails." Here the fallacy rests upon a punning interpretation of "no."

Proving the Wrong Conclusion, in which the attempt to confuse conclusions is made, with the result that some people will imagine that the case is established. Jevons says: "This was the device of the Irishman, who was charged with theft on the evidence of three witnesses, who had seen him do it; he proposed to call thirty witnesses who had not seen him do it. Equally logical was the defense of the man who was called a materialist, and who replied, 'I am not a materialist; I am a barber.'"

Fallacy of Unsuccessful Argument, in which is attempted the illogical conclusion that because a certain argument has failed the opposite conclusion is proven. This fallacy is quite common, especially in cases of juries. One side fails to prove certain contentions, and the jury leaps to the conclusion that the opposite contention must be correct. This is clearly fallacious, for there is always the possibility of a third explanation. In the case of a claim of alibi juries are apt to fall into this fallacy. The failure of the attempt to establish an alibi is often held to be in the nature of proof of the guilt of the accused. Old trial lawyers assert that a failure to establish a claimed alibi tends to injure the chance of the accused more than direct evidence against him. Yet, as all logical reasoners will see, there is no logical validity in any such inference. As Jevons has well said: "No number of failures in attempting to prove a proposition really disprove it." At the end of each failure the case simply stands in the same position as before the attempt; i.e., "not proven."

All Violations of the Rules of the Syllogism constitute fallacies, as may be seen by forming a syllogism in violation of one or more of the rules.

The logicians, particularly those of ancient times, took great pains to discover and name new variations of fallacies, many of which were hair-splitting in nature, and not worthy of being considered seriously. Some of those which we have enumerated may possibly be open to the same criticism, but we have omitted many of the worst offenders against practical common sense. An understanding of the fundamental Laws of Reasoning is sufficient to expose and unmask all fallacies, and such understanding is far more valuable than the memorizing of the names of hair-splitting fallacies which would not deceive a child.

In addition to the above stated fallacies of Deductive Reasoning, there are other fallacies which are met with in Inductive Reasoning. Let us briefly consider them.

Hasty and False Generalization is a common fallacy of this class. Persons sometimes see certain qualities in a few individuals of a class, and mistakenly infer that all the individuals in that class must possess these same qualities. Travelers frequently commit this fallacy. Englishmen visiting the United States for a few weeks have been known to publish books upon their return home making the most ridiculous generalizations regarding the American people, their assertions being based upon the observation of a few scattered individuals, often not at all representative. Americans traveling abroad commit similar errors. A flying trip through a country does not afford the proper opportunity for correct generalization. As Brooks says: "No hypothesis should be accepted as true until the facts are so numerous that there can be no doubt of its being proved."

Fallacies of Observation result from incorrect methods of observation among which may be mentioned the following: (1) Careless Observation, or inexact perception and conception; (2) Partial Observation, in which one observes only a part of the thing or fact, omitting the remainder, and thus forming an incomplete and imperfect concept of the thing or fact; (3) Neglect of Exceptions and Contradictory Facts, in which the exceptions and contradictory facts are ignored, thereby giving undue importance to the observed facts; (4) Assumption of Facts which are not real facts, or the assumption of the truth of things which are untrue; (5) Confusing of Inferences with Facts, which is most unwarrantable.

Fallacies of Mistaken Cause result from the assumption of a thing as a cause, when it is not so, of which the following are familiar examples: Substituting the Antecedent for the Cause, which consists in assuming a mere antecedent thing for a cause of another thing. Thus one might assume that the crowing of the cock was the cause of daybreak, because it preceded it; or that a comet was the cause of the plague which followed its appearance; or in the actual case in which a child reasoned that doctors caused deaths, because observation had shown that they always visited persons before they died; or that crops failed because a President of a certain political party had been inaugurated a few months before. Some fallacies of everyday reasoning are quite as illogical as those just mentioned. Substituting the Symptom for the Cause, which consists in assuming as a cause some mere symptom, sign or incident of the real cause. To assume that the pimples of measles were the cause of the disease, would be to commit a fallacy of this kind. We have mentioned elsewhere the fallacy which would assume silk-hats to be the cause of Civilization, instead of being a mere incident of the latter. Politicians are fond of assuming certain incidents or signs of a period, as being the causes of the prosperity, culture and advancement of the period, or the reverse. One might argue, with equal force, that automobiles were the causes of national prosperity, pointing to the fact that the more automobiles to be seen the better the times. Or, that straw hats produced hot weather, for similar reasons.

The Fallacy of Analogy consists in assuming a resemblance or identity, where none exists. We have spoken of this in another chapter. Brooks says, also: "It is a fallacy to carry an analogy too far; as to infer from the parable of the praying of the importunate woman that God resembles the unjust judge."

In conclusion, we would call your attention to the following words from Jevons, in which he expresses the gist of the matter: "It is impossible too often to remind people that, on the one hand, all correct reasoning consists in substituting like things for like things, and inferring that what is true of one will be true of all which are similar to it in the points of resemblance concerned in the matter. On the other hand, all incorrect reasoning consists in putting one thing for another where there is not the requisite likeness. It is the purpose of the rules of deductive and inductive logic to enable us to judge as far as possible when we are thus rightly or wrongly reasoning from some things to others."

FINIS

Check our website often for free ebook offers from
time to time AND we are
continually adding more titles!
240+ Book Titles & Counting!

Mel & Wen's
Life Transformation Publishing
www.lifetransformationpublishing.com
2016

Specializing in Transforming Lives!

36678520R00072

Printed in Great Britain
by Amazon